Attracting & Rewarding Outstanding Employees

Entrepreneur. MAGAZINE'S **Expert***Advice*

Attracting & Rewarding Outstanding Employees

DAVID RYE

EP
Entrepreneur. Press

Editorial Director: Jere Calmes
Cover Design: Dunn and Associates
Composition and Production: Eliot House Productions

This publication is designed to provide accurate and authoritative information in regard to the subject matter covered. It is sold with the understanding that the publisher is not engaged in rendering legal, accounting, or other professional services. If legal advice or other expert assistance is required, the services of a competent professional person should be sought.

Library of Congress Cataloging-in-Publication Data
Rye, David E.
    Attracting and rewarding outstanding employees/David Rye.
       p. cm.
    Includes index.
    ISBN 1-891984-30-6
       1. Employees—Recruiting. 2. Employment interviewing. 3. Employee motivation. 4. Incentive awards. 5. Employees—Rating of. 6. Performance awards. 7. Employee retention. I. Title: At head of title: Entrepreneur magazine's expert advice. II. Entrepreneur (Santa Monica, Calif.) III. Title.
    HF5549.5.R44 R93 2002
    658.3'142—dc21   2001023240

Printed in Canada
09 08 07 06 05 04 03 02 01 10 9 8 7 6 5 4 3 2 1

CONTENTS

PREFACE

FOR MOST ENTREPRENEURS, SUCCESS IS NOT ACHIEVED ALONE. Sure, you are responsible for the things you have accomplished. You provided the leadership, inspiration, and drive to build your business. But somewhere along the way, you had to rely on others.

You needed not just good employees, but outstanding employees to help make it happen.

Running a business today is certainly different than it was a decade ago. Competition is more fierce, and human resources are less plentiful. When you hire the people you need to run your business, you have to make more creative use of them to maximize the return on your investment. On top of that, the risk of losing outstanding employees, even when you think you have them well in hand, is an on-going concern.

How do you define an outstanding employee? A good employee is just better than average. An outstanding employee is the best of the breed. They're in the top ten percent of the labor force. Some are considered outstanding because of their technical expertise. Others are valued for their dedication, productivity, drive, determination, creative capacity, or leadership.

In this book, you'll discover a smorgasbord of ideas to help you seek out, find, and retain outstanding employees. You'll eagerly consume some of these ideas while others may not be what you are looking for right now. Feel free to pick and choose. If you find one good idea that makes a significant difference in your organization, then your investment in this book will be worth it.

INTRODUCTION

A TTRACTING, RECRUITING, AND RETAINING EMPLOYEES HAS become a critical challenge for entrepreneurs. *Attracting & Rewarding Outstanding Employees* is chock-full of information, ideas, and insights on how you can do it. This book deals with questions you can use to discover just what constitutes an outstanding employee for your particular organization. Follow-up questions address where to find and how to recruit outstanding employees. Plenty of help is offered along the way, including numerous "real world" examples and illustrations to show you how to make it all happen.

Once you hire an outstanding employees, how do you keep them? You spend a lot of time and money finding the right employees. How do you protect your investment? These and other related questions are addressed, and the guidance will provide you with a wealth of ideas on what you can do to reward your employees and keep them perpetually motivated. You decide which approaches would be most effective for your organization.

In this book, you will find several methods of highlighting important tips and supplemental information. These short asides are designed to help you focus on important ideas that deserve a little more attention. Here's a description of these boxed tips and sidebars:

IN*sight*

These boxes are designed to give you another perspective on the principles and practices covered in a chapter. By providing you with an example or an analogy, the insight box can help you focus on alternative strategies.

WARNING

Mistakes are always possible when executing a hiring program. These boxes alert you to what might go wrong and how to minimize mistakes.

PLAN OF ACTION

These boxes direct you to specific steps you might want to include in your action plan.

HOW TO

Use these ideas to simplify the task of recruiting and retaining outstanding employees in your organization.

SIDEBARS

Sidebars have also been included throughout the book that cover relevant and interesting material that pertains to the topics in the chapter. Here's an example of what a sidebar looks like:

Tom Peters put the right spin on the word "mistake" when he said, "The essence of innovation is the pursuit of failure, and one's ability to try different things and not be concerned about making mistakes. The assumption that all great leaders shared is that we all need to experiment, innovate, and be daring in our thinking. You can't be innovative and not make mistakes."

1

WHAT IS AN OUTSTANDING EMPLOYEE?

W HAT'S THE BEST WAY FOR YOUR ORGANIZATION TO SUCCEED IN today's tough business environment? Hire outstanding employees to support your outstanding management team. You need people who are capable of achieving your organization's goals and objectives—people with superb knowledge and skills, great aptitudes, and achievement attitudes.

A good team will always get assigned tasks done in time. An outstanding team will get all assigned tasks done in record time and fulfill all your organizational goals and objectives. It doesn't matter whether you're running a manufacturing company, service business, professional firm, or educational institution. The need for outstanding employees in any business is universal.

WHAT ARE THE QUALITIES OF OUTSTANDING EMPLOYEES?

Outstanding employees are those capable of accomplishing tasks far beyond the scope of most other employees. This is why you want to attract and recruit them into your organization. Your outstanding people are in the top 10 percent of your work force. Once you've successfully recruited them, your next challenge will be to enable these employees to be as productive as possible and to keep them from leaving your team.

What makes employees perform at outstanding levels? It doesn't necessarily require any particular level of education or professional credentials. We all know that experience doesn't automatically make people better employees. Outstanding employees know how to apply what they have learned to successfully complete any job you assign them. The speed with which they complete the job doesn't necessarily make any difference to them. If speed compromises quality, they'll drive for quality first. They know how to leverage their strengths and minimize their weaknesses to get the job done.

DON'T RUSH THE NET

Perhaps you've watched Chris Evert play tennis. Then you know this number-one world-ranked player could have improved her game by rushing to the net more often. Yet she chose not to work on this part of her game. Evert knew that she couldn't be good at everything, and she didn't try to be. Knowing her strengths and weaknesses, she defied conventional wisdom by working on her strong points first, then on her weak points only when she had time.

Look at outstanding employees in any business, and you'll realize they aren't good at everything they do. They're usually great at a few things, which they apply to get the job done. Chris Evert became the number-one tennis player in the world by concentrating on perfecting and utilizing her strengths, before she worked on improving her weaknesses.

In some organizations, it's the creative employee that's considered. In others, it is the one who can stick with a tough project and see it through to a successful completion. Some employees are considered outstanding because they communicate and work well with others. Others are valued because they work independently and get the job done.

The assessment of an outstanding employee is a value judgment you have to make. You must determine which of your employees are the more valued members of your team. They're your pacesetters. As pacesetters, they inspire and motivate others in your organization through their example and enthusiasm. Finding the right team members will make a significant difference in the overall success of your organization.

UNDERSTAND EMPLOYEES BASIC NEEDS

Like everyone, outstanding employees have a basic set of needs. Once you understand and appreciate these needs, you'll stand a better chance of attracting and keeping outstanding people in your organization. Psychologists have struggled for years to explain basic human needs. One of the most helpful explanations is Abraham Maslow's hierarchy of needs, which ranks all needs from low to high (see illustration).

MASLOW'S HIERARCHY OF NEEDS

Self-actualization

Self esteem

Social needs

Safety and security needs

Physiological needs

He explained that people will strive to satisfy lower-level needs first, before they focus on satisfying higher-level needs.

Maslow's Hierarchy of Needs and Employee Behavior

How does Maslow's hierarchy of needs influence an outstanding employee's behavior? Physiological needs such as air, food, and water took precedence on Maslow's list. Most of us have fortunately been able to meet these needs, or we wouldn't be alive today.

Safety needs are next on the list and include feeling secure in one's physical, emotional, and financial welfare. This becomes relevant when searching for an outstanding employee. Suppose you have found a potentially outstanding employee who is concerned about his health, personal life, or credit issues and financial well-being. These distractions could keep him from performing as an outstanding employee.

Once someone passes the safety and security needs hurdle, fulfilling social needs becomes a priority. Close relationships with friends, spouse, family, and fellow employees are increasingly important. Most people have a strong need to be accepted and belong to a team. Employees who don't have their social needs met won't produce at anywhere near an outstanding level.

Once people fulfill their social needs, they'll seek out ways to meet their self-esteem needs. Now, they are concerned about self-concept, confidence in personal strengths, and status, reputation, and recognition in the organization. People with high self-esteem can usually help build others' self-esteem in the organization. To find out about potential employees' self-esteem, ask questions such as: "Tell me about your strengths?" "What are your weaknesses?" "Do you have a good reputation among your peers?" "Are there things others don't like about you?"

Self-actualization, the need to realize one's full potential, is at the top of Maslow's needs list. Self-actualization needs are motivated by a sense of making a significant contribution to an organization and attaining a high level of self-worth. They're what motivate employees to achieve all they are capable of, a primary component of outstanding performers. People who feel good about themselves are motivated to achieve worthwhile objectives that validate the purpose of their lives.

In summary, outstanding employees have control over all their basic needs. Since outstanding employees tend to be perfectionists, they will continue to work toward higher levels of achievement, even once their basic needs are met.

LEARN ABOUT A CANDIDATE'S INTERPERSONAL RELATIONSHIPS

We often overlook asking about someone's interpersonal relationships. Perhaps we are afraid of infringing on a person's private life. However, people can have all the outstanding qualifications in the world, but without good interpersonal relationships, they are not going to perform well on the job. Don't be afraid to ask questions that might uncover interpersonal problems like: "How do you and your current boss get along?."

What Else Do Employees Need?

Employees need feedback on their work. You have an obligation to your employees to individually recognize their achievements and progress toward agreed-upon goals. Are you satisfied with their progress? If not, tell them why so that they will know how to improve.

Employees need to be involved in designing and establishing goals for a particular job. Your outstanding employees will have specific ideas about how things should be done and will openly question why certain things are not done. Listen to and involve them. In fact, it is good to encourage all your employees to become more actively involved in their jobs.

Some employees may need your help in resolving personal problems. This doesn't mean you have to become a full-time social worker.

SEEK OUTSIDE HELP

In some cases, it may be appropriate to seek outside help when dealing with your employees' personal problems. This could include helping them gain access to substance abuse centers, psychiatric facilities, or special counseling services. Make sure they agree to any proposed action you take before you proceed.

But it does suggest you should count on investing some of your time advising, counseling, and coaching your people. Be sensitive and understanding as you help them with their personal problems.

ARE YOUR EMPLOYEES PASSIONATE?

Employees who bring lots of passion to work are likely to be superlative and outstanding performers who can consistently drive your business forward. They love what they are doing. There are three different types of passion to look for when scouting for outstanding employees:

1. Passion for your company
2. Passion for the industry
3. Passion for your organization's career opportunities

Employees who have a lot of passion in one of these areas but express little for the others will circumvent their performance ability. For example, if they like the industry and their job, but not your company, you will surely lose them to a competitor. Even it they apply for your job, they'll probably decide they don't want it. There are several questions you can ask to rate a person's passion.

Does the Person Like Your Company?

Ask what they like or don't like about your company's products and services. What other aspect of your company do they like or not like? If you're running a start-up company, will they fit in with the entrepreneurial mind-set of other staff members? If your company is more structured and bureaucratic, will they be happy in that environment? Find out what type of work environments they like and don't like. Then determine if their likes match your environment.

WARNING

A candidate who has done no research on your company is probably not interested in the job.

Are They Excited about the Industry?

When you ask if they are excited about the industry, watch out for canned answers such as, "I see computer chips as being the industry of the future." Their response should be based on both work experience and personal values. Have they taken the time to study the companies, products, and services that are in the industry? Can they articulate why they believe the industry holds promise? What is it that excites them about the industry?

Do They Have Strong Personal Interests?

People with strong personal interests generally lead more balanced lifestyles and can recharge their batteries faster than those with limited interests. The types of activities people enjoy in their spare time may give you further insights into how they might approach work-related issues. Do they excel in one or two activities, or do they like to experiment with a broad variety?

Look for an ongoing commitment to a hobby or sport; this is a common characteristic in outstanding employees. Ask questions such as, "Tell me about your involvement in activities outside of work over the last several years?" These may include civic and political activities, professional and nonprofessional associations, reading, sports, and hobbies.

Do They Live a Balanced Lifestyle?

A workaholic is a classic example of an employee who does not enjoy a balanced lifestyle. Such people seldom fit the mold of an outstanding employee. Don't be afraid to ask the question "Are you able to balance your personal life with your professional life?" You're looking for a person who can juggle work and outside activities without overextending themselves. People who have well-rounded lifestyles are less likely to burn out from a demanding job. They're capable of giving sufficient attention to both work and their outside activities without upsetting the balance. They also know how to quickly respond to changing circumstances that may demand a disproportionate amount of time at work at the expense of their outside activities.

ALL WORK AND NO PLAY

Don't hire workaholics. Workaholics use work as an excuse to escape from their personal life. They're always scurrying around trying to keep busy and convince others they are indispensable. Workaholics are driven by a fear of failure that's based on low self-esteem. As a result, they never become outstanding employees. Outstanding employees know how to measure what they do against what it costs and balance their personal and professional lives.

Are They Creative?

Your decision to move particular employees up through the ranks of your organization rests in part with your conviction that they're creative. In a structured organization, you may be able to get by with uncreative employees. But in an entrepreneurial organization, employees must be creative if they are to achieve outstanding levels of performance. Find out about candidates' potential creativity by asking the question:"What's the most creative and innovative idea you've ever had?" Listen carefully to the answer. Can they demonstrate that they have creative ideas that will work well within your organization?

NEVER GIVE UP!

Thomas Edison is a classic example of someone who was driven by creativity. He knew exactly where he wanted to go, what he wanted to do, and how he was going to get there. While he was in the process of becoming an inventor, a young reporter asked, "Mr. Edison, how does it feel to have failed 10,000 times in your light bulb venture?" Edison replied, "Young man, I have not failed 10,000 times as you suggest. I have successfully found 10,000 ways that will not work." Edison estimated that he actually performed over 14,000 experiments while inventing the light bulb.

Can They Do the Job?

You can usually determine quickly whether or not employees have the basic skills to do a job. But even when they do, they may perform these skills quite differently than others. Probe candidates with questions to gain insight into how they will perform. For example, ask them: "What skills do you think are most critical for this job? Can you elaborate on the skills that make you the perfect candidate?"

Can They Solve Problems?

Many people try to skirt problem issues or downplay their significance. Outstanding employees are those who are willing to talk freely about problems and explain what they have done to solve those problems. If they talk defensively about how they've handled specific problems, you're probably dealing with someone who will inundate you with other peoples' problems every chance they get. Ask them to tell you about a major problem they helped resolve. If they can explain what they did and how they successfully worked with others, then you have candidates with the potential to be outstanding employees.

Do They Have Any Hidden Problems?

How do you find out about hidden problems? At the end of an interview, ask the question "Do you really want this job?" You are essentially asking candidates to make one last sales pitch for themselves. Watch their body language carefully. If their eyes are shifting and their body is fidgeting, they probably don't want the job. Now is the time to address any last-minute concerns. You may have discussed several sensitive issues during the conversation. Maintain your cool regardless of how you may feel about any negative answers you received.

INsight

If candidates can't tell you with conviction why they want the job,
then they probably aren't interested.

DO THEY POSSESS STRONG LEADERSHIP QUALITIES?

Leadership abilities are not optional for someone you want to promote to manager or team leader in today's dynamic organization. A person may know how to manage, but if he can't lead people to higher levels of achievement, he won't last long. Almost anybody can learn how to manage, but only a few can learn to become exceptional leaders.

Certainly, many outstanding employees may not have a desire to move into management positions. But how do you measure the leadership abilities of those who aspire to move up through your organization? Ask them the question "How would your associates describe your leadership style?" Look for a response that indicates they know what leadership is and how best to apply it in your organization.

Can They Pass the Leadership Test?

The word "leadership" didn't even enter into the English language until the early 1800s, and even then nobody knew what it meant. It was another 100 years before social scientists undertook serious studies about the phenomenon of leadership. Only in the past 40 years have researchers been able to make up for the lost time by studying how people become effective leaders. Many of these studies provide amazingly consistent findings about what constitutes a good leader. These findings are summarized as follows:

- Leaders listen with understanding, are always willing to discuss problems, and are open to any new ideas.
- Leaders offer support and help. You can count on them to back you up when necessary.
- Leaders know how to use the team approach to solve difficult problems. They are excellent facilitators.
- Leaders avoid close supervision and are not micromanagers. They do not dictate or rule by the book.
- Leaders are not afraid to delegate authority, rely on other peoples' judgment, and have faith in the creativity of others.
- Leaders communicate openly and honestly. You can trust what they say.
- Leaders bring out the best in employees and are in constant touch with them.
- Leaders always work toward increasing inter organizational cooperation.
- Leaders are always on the lookout for ways to increase productivity, reduce costs, and increase profits.
- Leaders know how to plan and set goals that people can relate to.

LEADERS ARE BORN AND NOT MADE

That's what most social scientists thought before they started their serious investigation of leadership 40 years ago. Prior to that, strong social class barriers made it next to impossible for anyone to become a leader unless the position was inherited. If your name wasn't Rockefeller, Firestone, or Rothchild, you were not destined to become a leader. It wasn't until class barriers began to crumble that people from all stations of society started becoming leaders. Only then did people begin to realize that leadership requires much more than being born into the right family.

CAN YOU MEET THEIR CAREER ASPIRATIONS?

Once you attract and hire outstanding employees, how do you keep them? How long are they going to stay with your organization before they get a better offer from a competitor? These are nagging questions that you must address. You definitely don't want employees to work in a position they don't like. Nor do you want individuals who complain all the time. If they don't like the job, they'll just show up to work to collect a paycheck. Or, they'll find another job.

Before you hire them, ask your potentially outstanding candidates the question

"Where do you want to be in five years?"

A well-thought-out answer should include a plan that demonstrates how they will achieve responsibility but not emphasize job titles or pay structures. Have they done their homework on your company and the industry to learn how they fit into their career aspirations? Does their plan indicate a logical path of upward mobility that you can accommodate?

SUMMARY

When you wrap up your interviews with candidates or fact-finding conversations with employees, always end on a positive note. Make sure they are satisfied with all your answers to their questions. Ask them "Did I answer all of your questions to your satisfaction?" Don't be afraid to ask them if they are interested in the job. That way if they are not, you can go on to your next candidate.

HOW DO YOU BEAT THE COMPETITION?

E ARLIER IT WAS MENTIONED THAT IF YOU WANT TO RUN AN OUT-standing organization, then you must hire outstanding people. Your competitors also know this and will invest thousands of dollars to recruit and attract top notch candidates. They'll aggressively seek the people they need, including the ones who work for you, to meet their quotas.

Unfortunately, the situation has gotten worse in the tight labor market of the new millennium. We can no longer expect superior candidates to come knocking at our door. We all know we can find outstanding people on college campuses, in high schools and vocational schools, and working for other employers. But what can you do to attract them? What steps do you need to take to stay ahead of your competition?

- *Constantly address your employees' needs.* Never assume that every one of your employees is satisfied with her job. Ask her the question "How are you doing today?" If she says, "Okay, I guess," find out what's wrong.

- *Create and share a common vision.* Once you create a vision, ask employees what they think and if they're excited about it. If you have to constantly remind them about what the vision is, then maybe it doesn't mean anything to them.

- *Always work together as a team in both good and bad situations.* Let your people know that you will back them all the way to the edge of a cliff if that is what it takes to resolve a situation.

- *Build loyalty in the relationship.* Do this by keeping your word on every promise you make. If you are not sure you can keep a promise, then qualify your commitment. For example, there is nothing wrong with telling a person "Let me see what I can do and I will get back to you tomorrow." You haven't committed yourself, but you have assured the person that you will try.

- *Fuel enthusiasm by keeping your people motivated.* You do this by constantly demonstrating your own motivation in everything you do. Show them how to treat problems not as problems, but rather as exciting challenges. Help them find solutions to their problems.

- *Encourage them to take risks without risking their job.* As the old saying goes, the person who never makes a decision never makes a mistake. Teach and convince your people that making mistakes is a critical part of building a viable business, as long as you learn from each mistake.

- *Propagate honesty in your corporate culture.* If you don't instill honesty throughout your organization, then you are running with a pack of thieves. Whatever you do or say is subject to the whims and desires of every dishonest person in your charge.

CAN YOU OFFER EMPLOYEES STABILITY?

College, vocational, and high school graduates are always anxious to discuss job opportunities with employers who are hungry for their talent and energy. Unfortunately, they'll often respond to high salary offers that make them look good in the eyes of their peers. But if you take the time to really quiz outstanding employees, you'll discover that many are more concerned about stability, the quality of a company, and personal growth opportunities. There's a shift toward wanting stability as America's young people search for security in their lives. Can your organization offer new graduates a stable work environment that your competitors can't match?

PLAN OF ACTION

Recruiting people employed by other companies has become increasingly difficult because most employers are trying desperately to hang onto their best people. If you want to hire outstanding people, you must show them there are significant advantages to making a career change.

Create a Company Profile

One way to demonstrate your company's stability to candidates is to show a company portfolio. Invite them to make copies of any sections that interest them. Your portfolio might include annual reports, news

---

WARNING

An unstable work environment, where the fear of losing one's job is a nagging concern, could make all your vision statements meaningless. A vision implies a future for the company, which contradicts an unstable work environment.

---

releases about company accomplishments, a brief history of the company, or any other material that demonstrates stability.

How Do You Offer Stability?

A stable organization is one that is willing to change. You can influence worker productivity and job satisfaction by the degree of stability and risk your organization offers. Although risk implies the opposite of stability, both terms can be comfortably present in the same organization. The concept of risk goes hand in hand with change. Organizational change has become a fact of life. If you're not willing to change, then the stability of your organization is at risk.

Now, having said all that, if you can show your people and anyone who is interested in working for your organization why you have a stable organization and how you plan to keep it stable, you will be one giant step ahead of your competitors. Why? Most of them do not address stability issues with their people. That's a mistake because you had better believe that the issues are on the minds of their workers. If the turnover figures are low, show the numbers to prospective employees.

HOW DO YOU ATTRACT COMPETITORS' EMPLOYEES?

It is increasingly difficult to recruit people from the ranks of your competitors. More companies are now embracing unique programs like employee stock options. If you expect to entice someone to make a career change, you'll have to be able to demonstrate the decided advantages of joining your organization. One of the ways you do that is by mounting a well-coordinated public relations campaign that enhances your corporate image.

Start by broadcasting positive messages about your company. Strive to gain media exposure by supporting charitable causes, United Way fund drives and urban redevelopment programs. Don't concentrate on just the big stories. Even things like sponsoring a Little League team boost your company's image as a good employer. Publicly announce employee promotions and significant accomplishments, such as new discoveries, inventions, and patents. If one of your people is elected to a trade or professional association, recognize the achievement inside your organization and place an article in your local newspaper.

THE GOLDEN RULE OF RECRUITING

There are "rules of the road" that you should obey when you recruit employees from competitors. They fall under the Golden Rule: "Do unto others as you would have others do unto you." Never recruit candidates at their work place. This includes personal visits or telephone calls. Meet with them at an independent site and call them at home. If you violate the "rules of the road," be prepared to experience the same illicit recruiting practices by your competitors.

WHAT'S IN IT FOR ME?

Although you may not like it, more employees are asking the question: "What's in it for me if I join your organization?" If they don't see the positive aspects of working for you, they're history. To attract outstanding people, you must have something to offer them. If they don't believe your organization offers better career opportunities than their current position, they won't make the move.

Your company must be a great place to work with a comfortable environment, produce quality products and services, and enjoy an excellent reputation if you expect to attract and keep outstanding employees. If you can show candidates that you are a solid company with a clear sense of the future, they'll join your organization.

Do You Have a Mission?

If you don't have a company mission, create one. Invite your employees to help you put a mission statement together so that they can relate to it. Organizational missions are shared conceptions of the organization's intention, purpose, or objectives. Your mission may be included in a policy statement or printed on the back of employee business cards.

Missions are often stated in very broad terms and are sometimes called purpose statements. A good mission statement addresses why an organization exists and what it's trying to accomplish. Here's an example of a mission statement that was developed at Western Industries, a long-established manufacturing firm. It's printed on the back of every employee's business card and reads "Our mission is to become the market leader in the production and distribution of heavy extraction equipment."

To achieve this mission, Western created a number of goals designed to increase its market share of dump truck sales by 20 percent. Explaining its mission statement to employees and potential employees put Western in a much better position to establish work priorities that were in alignment with the goals of the company.

What's Unique about Your Company?

Why should someone want to work for you instead of a competitor? What makes your organization unique and more attractive than the other organizations that are in your industry? Rest assured that outstanding candidates are going to meticulously compare your offer with any other offer they receive. It's one thing to tell a candidate about all of the things your company has accomplished, but it is quite another to be able to show them. Put pictures, certificates of accomplishments, and anything else that's relevant on the walls throughout your facility. When you and your candidate take a tour of the facility, proudly point out some of the wall hangings. Your candidate will begin to realize what a great company you have.

Create a Picture

A picture is still worth a thousand words. If you don't have a scrapbook full of company news articles and testimonials, then make one. Be sure it's bound in a quality leather binder so that when you hand it to candidates, they'll know they are reviewing a quality document. Include pictures of your employees attending company picnics, Christmas parties, and special events to show that you are a people-oriented company. Also include any newspaper or magazine articles that announce something special about your company.

SUMMARY

Remember that the theme of this chapter is beating your competition. How do you keep them from stealing your outstanding people? How do you attract outstanding people away from your competition? It should be clear to you by now that you do it by creating an outstanding organization, one that people are proud to be a part of. Candidates that you interview will immediately recognize this; the people who work for you will already know it.

WHERE DO YOU FIND OUTSTANDING EMPLOYEES?

T HE *WIZARD OF OZ* WAS TRULY AN INSPIRING MOVIE, EVEN FOR adults. All Dorothy had to do was follow the Yellow Brick Road and she would get to Oz, where all her dreams would come true. The movie reminds me of the job market in the 1990s, when it was relatively easy to find outstanding employees if you just followed the Yellow Brick Road and placed a few simple ads here and there.

Now that the 1990s are behind us, I'm sure you've noticed that the Yellow Brick Road has been torn up and replaced with a new speedway. Good people, let alone outstanding people, are harder and harder to find since the labor market tightened up in the late 1990s. Competition has grown fierce as companies struggle to create new and exciting programs that will attract employees. Outstanding people today are also smarter than ever. They are well connected into the Internet and know exactly what's out there and where they want to go.

————————————— WARNING ——————————————

Don't take for granted that your best workers will stay with you. If you want to keep them, continue to reinforce their value and the opportunities they have in your organization. If you begin to take employees for granted, you open your door to your competitors to come in and take them.

CREATE AN EXCITING JOB DESCRIPTION

The job title heads and your job description can produce favorable or unfavorable responses all by themselves. Don't underestimate their importance. Choose a title that reflects the most important overall responsibilities of the position. Suppose you have a sales position that you are trying to fill. The job description heading could read "Sales Person" or "Sales Account Executive." Which one would get your attention? Hopefully, it's the second one.

Be specific. Avoid generalizations in a job description so you can match the job requirements to the ideal candidate. Focus on one or two key job responsibilities, and summarize them in one short but concise sentence. Knowledge, skill, and experience requirements should be precisely conveyed in the ad to discourage unqualified applicants. If there are a number of responsibilities or background requirements that go with the job, use bulleted lists to make the ad easier to read. Bullets can also make your ad more noticeable. Be clear and concise.

HOW DO YOU ATTRACT OUTSTANDING PEOPLE?

The things you do to make your firm appealing to potential employees are prerequisites to getting people to apply for a job with your organization. You need to create an image that makes your organization look good as an employer. There are numerous ways to spread the positive word about employment with your company. Personnel staffs usually think first about displays and interviews on college campuses and at trade or vocational shows. That's OK for targeted efforts, but your company still needs a positive image to support one-on-one recruiting efforts. Mount a public relations campaign and use the news media to spread the word of your company accomplishments.

Newspaper Advertising

It is sometimes taken for granted that you'll place a help-wanted classified ad when you want to hire someone. However, as we have already warned, you rarely get attention by placing "vanilla" classifieds. Outstanding candidates will quickly sift through and discard them as if they were junk mail.

Creating a classified ad is relatively straightforward. Start with an exciting job title at the top of the ad. Include the name of your business followed by a brief description of the challenges of the job along with duties and responsibilities. Next, state what the ideal candidate looks like in terms of qualifications, experience, and education. Include company contact information such as its mailing address, e-mail address, and fax and telephone numbers at the bottom of the ad.

SAMPLE CLASSIFIED AD FOR AN OFFICE MANAGER

State-of-the-art consulting firm seeks a dynamic Office Manager to take charge of our accounting, inventory, and purchasing functions. Excellent salary and potential for upward mobility in a rapidly growing company. Send your résumé to Western Solutions, PO Box 3475, Scottsdale, AZ 85258.

SAMPLE CLASSIFIED AD FOR A DESKTOP PUBLISHER

Leading publishing firm has a full-time opening in our Graphics Communications Department for a "top-notch" desktop publisher. Experience required in Windows 2000, Quark Express, PageMaker, and Corel Draw. We offer great benefits and career growth opportunities to the right candidate. Send your résumé to Western Publications, PO Box 3475, Scottsdale, AZ 85258.

Online Advertising

The Adams Media World Wide Web site www.career.com offers employers an opportunity to post job listings for free. The site provides up-to-date career information for both employers and applicants, as well. It features a database that allows employers to search for appli-

SAMPLE ONLINE JOB POSTING

Job Code: If you respond to this job offer, please reference job code # 874566

Job Title: Cost Accountant

Job Location: Scottsdale, AZ

Job Description: Western Publications is a leader in outdoor books and is seeking an accounting professional to join our financial staff. Duties include tracking project financial performance and preparing project budgets and status reports.

Qualifications: College degree in accounting or finance with a minimum of two years in project-based accounting or a related field.

Benefits: We offer a salary commensurate with your experience, supplemented by an excellent benefit program. For more information about our company, visit our Web site www.WestpubsWorld.cs.

cants with specific qualifications. Applicants can also search for a specific type of job in a particular geographical location.

When you create an online classified ad, show the posting date when the ad was posted next to the job title. Many applicants want to know the job location, so make sure you include the city and state. A brief job description along with its qualifications and benefits, should follow. You may also want to include educational requirements, salary ranges, the starting dates, and the application closing date.

College Recruiting

College campuses are a great place to recruit young and energetic people who are more than eager to help you build a dynamic organization. Unfortunately, if you conduct a recruiting campaign on a pre-arranged recruiting day at a college, you are liable to find yourself competing with a hundred or more other organizations. In some cases, there may be more recruiters than there are candidates. How do you beat the odds?

Have you ever considered visiting your local college campus unannounced on a non-recruiting day? Here's how to do it! Arrive at the campus just before lunch and park yourself at the entrance to the student cafeteria. Arm yourself with plenty of company brochures, business cards, and a one-page descriptions of jobs that you're trying to fill. As students begin filing into the cafeteria, hand out the material. You'll be amazed at the positive reception you will receive. Vocational schools are also very receptive to this same approach.

HOW TO

Network with colleagues and peers in competing organizations via the telephone. Ask them for ideas on where to find outstanding candidates.

Offer Referral Rewards to Your Employees

We often overlook one of the best referral sources for outstanding employees: our own staff. Many of your employees have friends or former co-workers with outstanding credentials whom they could attract into your company. However, they may be reluctant to do so for fear that if the job they referred their friend to doesn't work out, they are at fault. To overcome this obstacle, put together an internal public relations campaign to encourage your employees to submit referrals. Here are several steps to include in your campaign:

- Offer a prize or monetary reward. A $100 reward paid, only when you hire the person who's referred to you, is a wonderful incentive.
- Ask your employees to help find the right person. Explain in a newsletter or company communication exactly what types of people you're looking for.
- Post open job positions. This way your employees can quickly determine if they know someone who is qualified for a position.

Pitch the stability of your company to your employees every day of the week. This will help overcome any anxiety they might have about encouraging a friend to apply for an open position. Openly share with employees why you believe your organization is a great place to work.

Look for Winners In Your Local Paper

Most major newspapers publish a "Who's Who" column in their business section. We've all seen them. "John Doe of the ABC Corporation was promoted to Director of Manufacturing" or "Sally Doe was nominated outstanding businesswoman of the year by the Scottsdale Chamber of Commerce." Most of these people are good, and many are outstanding.

Why not mount an active campaign to recruit such people who seem to fit your organization? Call and introduce yourself. Congratulate them on their achievement, and then ask the question "Do you know of anybody who might want a job with my company?" After you have told

---

WINNERS KNOW HOW TO WIN

Winners know how to exploit their full potential because they are always part of the answer to a problem. A loser is always part of the problem. A winner has goals. A loser has only excuses. A winner says, "Let me do it for you." A loser says, "That's not my job." Winners always see green near every sand trap. Losers only see sand. Only winners know how to win. They keep themselves motivated, are constantly learning new things, and respect everybody they work with.

---

them about the position you're trying to fill, sit back and see if they show any interest in interviewing for the position.

Work the Crowd at Meetings

It goes without saying that nobody knows what you're looking for if you don't tell them. Conversely, almost everybody in the business community knows someone who is searching for a job. We often attend business meetings, but seldom do we bring up our employee needs with those we're talking to. Perhaps it's because we think it is too private a matter to discuss with associates. This is wrong!

Make sure you ask the question "Hey Joe, I'm looking for an outstanding accountant. Do you know of anybody that I can talk to? If you find me someone, I'll take you out to lunch." In many cases, your associate will know of someone who meets your qualifications and be glad to give you a referral. The lunch option adds some icing on the cake.

IN*sight*

A personal referral is worth 100 random résumés.

HOLD AN OPEN HOUSE WITH PIZZAZZ

Anybody can hold an open house. You simply tell all of your employees and everybody else you know to come take a tour of your facility. When the open house day arrives and nobody shows up, you're left wondering what happened. You didn't hold an open house with pizzazz. What's pizzazz and how do you add it to your next open house? Few people will want to attend an open house to see your beautiful facility unless you offer some enticements. Offer guests an opportunity to meet your organization's key players or learn about your business plans or future business opportunities. If you offer good food and music, your guests will be extra happy they came.

Promoting Your Open House

Once you've planned the open house, your next step will be to mount a well-coordinated promotional campaign. Invite all your employees and encourage them to invite their friends. Make an exciting contest out of the event by holding a raffle and giving employees a raffle ticket that goes into a drawing bowl for every friend they bring. At the end of the event, whoever's ticket is drawn wins a prize, perhaps round-trip tickets for two to Hawaii. Promote the event in your local newspaper. Place fliers at area universities, colleges, and vocational and high schools. Contact your chamber of commerce and city government to see if you can get free publicity through their published bulletins.

SUMMARY

In many respects, finding outstanding candidates for a job is the most challenging aspect of the employee search process. The ideas covered in this chapter will help you get started. It's also important to ask for suggestions and ideas from anyone you know. You will be amazed at the great ideas people have that you might never have thought of.

HOW DO YOU PRESCREEN APPLICANTS?

N
O DOUBT YOU HAVE RUN A GREAT PROMOTIONAL CAMPAIGN and have more applicants than you will ever have time to see. Your next challenge is to quickly screen all of your candidates' applications and politely discard the one's you don't want. This way you can and concentrate on only the most outstanding candidates. This chapter discusses what to look for in a résumé and what questions to ask when considering candidates.

WHAT TO LOOK FOR IN A RÉSUMÉ

It's not uncommon for a single newspaper classified ad to pull in a hundred or more résumés. How do reduce that mass of paper to something that's more workable,31 like the top ten candidates? First, identify the top three to five minimum qualifications a candidate must have to fit your requirements. For example, if they must have a college education, then go through your pile of résumés and discard the ones that don't meet that requirement.

Weed your list down to the applicants you want to interview. You may want to conduct phone-screening interviews to determine your top five to ten candidates. After you have prioritized your candidates, look closely at their backgrounds to discover similarities and differences. Make a note of the questions you want to ask each candidate.

INsight

Spend a minimal amount of time screening out weak candidates so you can spend most of your time comparing the differences between your strongest candidates.

START BY ASKING THE RIGHT QUESTIONS

Asking the right question and getting the right answer is at the heart of any screening process. It's the only way to do it. According to *Webster's Dictionary*, a question is an interrogative expression often used to test a person's knowledge, or a subject or aspect in dispute or that is open to discussion. There are two basic ways to ask the right question.

First, you can ask yourself a question and come up with your own answer based upon the information that's available to you. For example, assume you have just read a candidate's résumé. If the résumé was properly prepared, you should be able to ask yourself a basic question "Does this candidate meet my minimal educational requirements?" If your answer is "No," the candidate goes into the "send them a not interested letter" pile and you can go on to the next application.

Second, you can ask a question directly to a candidate. During the screening stage, it is appropriate to call a candidate and ask a question

---

PLAN OF ACTION

Those who apply for a job with your organization but don't meet your qualifications deserve a "no thank you" letter. Sending them a post card doesn't cut it. Always protect the quality of your organization's image.

---

over the phone. You can even do it by e-mail. For example, assume that you have just reviewed a candidate's résumé. He appears to have the technical sales qualifications you're looking for, but you need more information. Call him and ask the question "Can you give me an example of a technical sale that you have recently closed?" Listen carefully. If he hesitates or starts to stutter, then you have your answer.

SAY "NO THANKS" PROFESSIONALLY

Rejection letters to unqualified candidates should be short, polite, and to the point. Send the same letter to every unqualified candidate to avoid any unfair labor practices. Here's an example of an acceptable paragraph: "Thank you for taking the time to apply to our recent job opening. Although your qualifications were excellent, we have found another candidate who more closely meets our requirements. We will keep your application on file for six months and contact you if your qualifications match any future openings we may have."

Ask Insightful Questions

During the interview, asking questions is the best way to gain insight and information that you need to strengthen your thoughts about a potentially outstanding candidate. Questions can also be used to help candidates gain an insight into your way of thinking. This should be one of your interview objectives. Suppose you're trying to find a new employee to assist you in implementing a major cost-cutting program. Before you present the specifics of what needs to be done, you might ask "Jim, do you believe that prudent cost cutting is critical to a growing organization?" If you get a "Yes" along with some qualified remarks, you are ready to introduce the specifics of your cost-cutting program. If your question elicits a "No," find out why Jim feels this way before you disclose the cost-cutting part of the job.

PLAN OF ACTION

Don't assume that all of your preferred candidates will accept a job offer from your organization. Make sure you ask them if they would be receptive to a job offer before you schedule follow-up interviews.

Open-Ended and Pinpoint Questions

Think of the question as an adjustable sales tool that you can employ during the interview. You can use open-ended questions to get a broad range of information or pinpoint questions to obtain more specific facts. Using different types of interview questions will help you learn more about a candidate's interest. An example of an open-ended question would be, "What do you think?" A narrow open-ended question might be, "Do you agree?" to solicit a "Yes" or "No" response.

Pinpoint questions might ask for a number, a reason, an opinion, or an explanation. For example, you might ask, "Do you believe it's possible for my organization to double its profits over the next twelve months?" Suppose you solicit a "Yes" response. Your follow-up in-between question might simply be "Tell me why?"

Introduction Question

Another kind of question to ask is one that introduces information that the candidate may not have considered. This type of interview

---

question can be used very effectively to change the direction of a candidate's thinking. A good starting introduction question might be "What if I could show you emperical numbers that would prove my point. Would that change your mind?" If the answer is "Yes," you can then present numbers for your listener to review. Another introduction question might be "Did you know that...?"

Raised Questions

Whenever you ask a question, it may raise another such as, "Why are you asking me that question?" It's human nature to be suspicious and some people want to know your reasoning before providing an answer. Whenever you ask a question, follow-up with "I'm asking this because I need more information." This clarifies why you're asking the question without giving an elaborate explanation.

EVERY QUESTION HAS A PURPOSE

As a general rule, it's best not to ask a question unless you know why you're asking it. If you don't know why, chances are the question isn't worth asking. Think about where you want your questions to lead before you ask them. Think of questions as qualifying tools used to help you get the information you need to make the right decision about a candidate. What are the answers you're hoping to get from an outstanding candidate?

QUESTIONS NOT TO ASK

If you think common sense is enough to keep your hiring practices legal, think again. Many of the legal issues that relate to hiring are not as straightforward as you might think. And, the legal issues apply not just to the person doing the hiring, but also to everyone involved in the hiring process. To further complicate matters, employment laws can change quickly.

───────────────────────── **WARNING** ─────────────────────────

*When in doubt about an employment law, contact an expert
like an employment attorney or a personnel expert.*

The following are the most commonly asked illegal questions. Similar questions may also have been deemed illegal, but because of the broad interpretations of the courts, it is impossible to list all of them.

Are You Married?

Many questions related to an applicant's sexual association are illegal, including marriage as strange as that may be. Suppose it's important to you to know if someone is married. Perhaps the job you want to fill will require a great deal of travel, which may be difficult for a married employee. Ask a question such as "Would your spouse like to take a tour of our facility?" You will then get the answer that you are looking for. Suppose your candidate says, "Thank you, but my spouse trusts my judgment and won't need to tour your facility." You can then ask the follow-up question, "Will your spouse have any problems adapting to the heavy travel schedule that this job demands?"

Do You Have Children?

It's illegal to ask an applicant about children since such questions can lead to discrimination against women. Assume you are trying to fill a job that will require an extensive amount of overtime. You have already disclosed this to the candidate you're interviewing, and they have told you they do not have a problem with excessive overtime. You might ask the question: "How will your family feel about the fact that you will often be working late at night?" Sit back and listen to their answer.

How Old Are You?

It's illegal to ask an applicant their age. The law was designed primarily to protect people over the age of 40. However, it's legal to ask an applicant if they are over 18. If they are not, you need to know because of federal, state, and local child labor laws. What's crazy about this law is that you can't ask someone how old they are in an interview, but you can ask for their date-of-birth on an employment application. You figure it out!

Did You Graduate from High School or College?

Believe it or not, you have to be careful when asking this question. To be safe, you must be able to demonstrate that the job requires a certain level of education for the question not to be considered discriminatory against someone with a low education level. If you include the minimum education requirement in the job ad or description, then you are OK. Again, what's crazy about this law is that although you can't legally ask someone what college or high school they attended during the interview, you can ask them for their educational background on the employment application.

Have You Ever Been Arrested?

The real question should be "Have you ever been convicted of a crime?" A person may have been arrested, but never convicted. In either event, you are well advised to not ask either question unless a person's past criminal record would have a direct bearing on the job position you are trying to fill. You can cover yourself by asking them to sign a form authorizing you to conduct a criminal background check. If they refuse, you probably have the answer to your question.

How Much Do You Weigh?

Avoid asking any question related to physical appearance. It has been ruled that such questions tend to discriminate against women and minorities. However there are exceptions, especially where safety is concerned. Suppose you are trying to fill a job in which a person's weight is a consideration. You're looking for a security guard who will be required to drive an electric vehicle throughout the compounds of your facility on a daily basis. The vehicle has a safety rating: Nobody over 250 pounds should drive the vehicle. In this case, you have an obligation to disclose such information to any candidate who may exceed the safety weight limit and ask if they are under that limit. Make sure this weight limit is covered in the job description.

What Country Are You From?

This question is clearly illegal because it discriminates against national origin. You can also get into trouble by asking an applicant what languages they speak, unless speaking a certain language is part of the job description. There are exceptions, however. Suppose you are trying to hire a person for a job that requires a security clearance from the U.S. government. In this case, they must be a U.S. citizen. If you have included this requirement in your job description, then you may ask "Based upon what I have told you, would you qualify for a security clearance from the U.S. government?"

Are You Handicapped?

You may not ask about an individual's possible handicaps. Furthermore, employers are generally required to make special accommodations for physically challenged employees. In many cases, you may actively be seeking to hire a disabled person, and this issue would not present a problem. However, if you're trying to fill a position that requires certain physical qualifications like standing for extended periods of time, it may be an issue. A person could have a subtle handicap like a bad hip or knee that would prevent them from performing this job. After you have explained the physical requirement of the job, ask the candidate "Can you think of any reasons why you would not be able to meet the physical demands of this job?"

ALWAYS LOOK FOR WINNERS

Finding winners to help you run your organization, whether it's a baseball team or a corporate team, is what makes the difference between winning or losing. Here is a list of guidelines on what it takes to be a winner, or conversely, what it takes to be a loser. Apply them as you search for outstanding job applicants.

- Winners make commitments and keep them. Losers makes promises and forget them.
- When winners make mistakes they say "I made a mistake" and correct the problem. When losers make mistakes they say "It wasn't my fault" and walk off.
- Winners work harder than losers, but have more free time because losers are always busy doing nothing.
- Winners go through a problem to solve it; losers go around it.
- Winners show they're sorry when they make a mistake by correcting it, while losers say "I'm sorry" and make the same mistake again.
- Winners listen before they speak. Losers just wait for their turn to say something without hearing what's being said.
- Winners say "There ought to be a better way." Losers say, "Why change the way we have always done it?"
- Winners respect and learn from people with more knowledge. Losers resent those who know more and criticize them behind their backs.
- Winners only know one speed: fast. Losers have two speeds: slow and stop.

- Winners have a realistic appreciation of their strengths and weaknesses. Losers are oblivious to any of their strengths and weaknesses.
- Winners learn from their mistakes. Losers avoid mistakes by not trying anything new or different.
- Winners are sensitive to other people's feelings. Losers are sensitive only to their own feelings.
- Winners are leaders and always show respect for other people. Losers lean on people who are stronger and take their frustrations out on those who are weaker.
- Winners admit to their prejudices and constantly work to correct them. Losers don't know how to correct anything.
- Winners know when to stop talking after they have made their point or the sale. Losers keep talking because they never know when they've made a point.
- Winners act the same toward those who are helpful and those who aren't because they know these same people may be helpful next time. Losers ignore anyone who can't be of immediate help.
- Winners know they can never stop learning, even when others consider them the experts. Losers think they already know everything.
- The saving grace of winners is their ability to laugh at themselves in a nondemeaning manner. Losers only know how to laugh at others.
- Winners are sympathetic to weaknesses in others because they understand their own weaknesses. Losers won't recognize any of their weaknesses.

INsight

"Winning isn't everything, but it sure beats whatever is second."

—Bear Bryant

• Winners know that in order to win, you have to be willing to give more than you take. Losers always take more than they give, even if it means stealing.

SUMMARY

Prescreening is a vital part of the search process for outstanding candidates. You don't have the time to personally interview every job applicant. You owe it to yourself and your organization to know as precisely as you can what you are looking for in terms of a candidate's education, experience, leadership qualities, and other relevant qualifications. Only then are you in a position to pass judgment on the applications you receive. If an applicant appears to meet your minimum expectations, then a telephone or face-to-face interview may be in order.

DON'T BE A CITY SLICKER

Do you remember in the movie *City Slickers* when Jack Palace told Billy Crystal, "There is only one thing that can cause your success in life." When Billy asked, "What's that?" Jack held up his finger as a gesture for him to seek the answer on his own. By the end of the movie, you hopefully discovered the answer. For the benefit of those of you who didn't see the movie, the answer was that under extreme circumstances every human being has the innate power to apply multiple skill levels that they didn't believe they had in order to win.

5

WHAT SHOULD YOU DO BEFORE THE INTERVIEW?

I T'S DURING THE ACTUAL INTERVIEW THAT YOU GET THE CHANCE TO know a candidate and ask more specific questions relevant to the job. Proper planning before the actual interview is critical if you want to get the most out of every interview minute you spend with a candidate. It is therefore important that you understand the various stages of the interview process and the objectives of each stage. These stages may be covered progressively in either a single interview or over several separate interviews depending upon the type of person you're looking for and your available time.

PREPARING FOR THE INTERVIEW

It's not unusual for a company to have three or even five interviews with a professional candidate before making a final decision. They may extend an offer after two or three interviews, then meet again if the candidate desires. The first interview is to ensure the candidate meets the basic job requirements. This is when you discuss the applicant's qualifications, skills, knowledge, leadership capabilities, motivation, and work style. It should take no longer than an hour and no less than a half hour. When you complete the initial interview, you should be in a position to either reject or pursue the candidate. You can then use follow-up interviews to compare each candidate's qualifications against the other applicants.

Predetermining a Candidate's Qualifications

How do you measure a candidate's qualifications, skills, knowledge, and experience? Start by preparing a list of questions directly related to the résumé. Ask probing questions that will help you analyze and measure whether or not a candidate meats your standards as a leader, team player, and communicator.

Review your job description and classified ad before the interview. Have information handy that the candidate might ask for, such as a copy of the job description, recruitment brochures, annual reports, and a summary of the company's benefits. Know how many people you plan to interview and when you want to complete your search. Are their any internal candidates you might want to consider? When do you want to fill this position?

Prepare Your Questions In Advance

Prepare in advance of each interview the questions you want to ask. Your first line of questions should relate to the candidate's résumé in terms of her qualifications, skills, and experience. Be prepared to ask her if she has work samples, transcripts, or references you can check to validate what's in her résumé.

Prepare a second set of questions that addresses her personal and professional qualifications. What leadership skills does she have? Is she highly motivated? Is she a team player or does she prefer to work alone? Is she a good communicator? You may get subjective answers to these questions, which makes them somewhat more difficult to access and analyze. If you don't understand her answer, continue to ask probing questions until you are satisfied. Your overall objective should be to determine whether a candidate measures up to your expectations for an outstanding employee.

Screening Candidates

Phone interviews are being used more and more as a tool to evaluate candidates before bringing them in for an interview. They save time and can help determine whether you want to arrange for a face-to-face meeting. Before you call a prospective candidate, make sure you have a clear agenda of the items you want to cover. Organize your questions in advance so that there will be a natural and orderly process to follow in your conversation. It is courteous to schedule a phone interview rather than assume the candidate will have the time to talk whenever you call. Be prepared to ask him the same direct qualifying questions that you would ask in person.

If the candidate doesn't sound right on the phone, chances are he won't sound any better when you meet. If this is the case, you've saved yourself a lot of time. Go on to your next candidate.

Set Up Interview Objectives

Your primary interview objective should be to determine the suitability of candidates who apply for the job. Be as thorough as possible evaluating a candidate's compatibility with your organization. Follow-up interviews usually occur when you have narrowed the field of applicants

> ### WARNING
>
> *The biggest disadvantage of telephone interviews is the lack of personal contact you have with the candidates. You cannot read their body language and eye movement, which often helps measure their level of enthusiasm. You don't know how they are physically reacting to your questions during a telephone interview.*

down to five or less. If your top candidates for the job are extremely close, you need to ask very specific questions. Be sure to ask each candidate the same questions so you can compare their answers and help determine who is best suited for the job.

Prepare a List of Structured Questions

Structured interview questions are standard ones that you ask all candidates. Such questions allow you to compare their answers and be fair and objective in your evaluation. These will also enable you to prioritize your candidates once you have concluded your first round of interviews. Structured questions you might want to ask include: "What are you strengths and weaknesses?" "Why should I hire you?" "What do you want to do in the immediate future?"

TEAM INTERVIEWS

Team interviews are an excellent way to get group consensus on several competing applicants. Save team interviews for your top candidates to minimize the time impact on your staff. The interview team may include managers from other departments and peer level employees

---

TRAIN YOUR INTERVIEWERS

Be sure anyone you involve in the interview process knows how to interview. Inexperienced interviewers must be trained; otherwise they may quickly turn away outstanding candidates. Interviewers should have at least a half day of training that includes instruction on how to ask the right questions, equal employment opportunity guidelines, and illegal questions. The interviewers must also know the job description well enough to be able to determine how a candidate will function in the job.

---

who can share their work experiences with a candidate. Set it up so they will be able to evaluate the candidate's qualifications and determine whether or not the applicant will fit in with the rest of the work team.

POSTING JOB OPENINGS

The internal posting of a job opening should be one of your first steps in the recruiting process. Let your employees know of any potential opening by placing an appropriate announcement and job description on a bulletin board. Let them know who they need to contact if they are interested in applying for the position.

If you use e-mail to announce company events, announce the job that way. Include the e-mail address of the person to contact if someone is interested in the job. Whatever method you use to post a job, make sure the information is available to all employees. You don't want an employee to come up to you after you've filled the position and tell you they didn't know it was available.

Internal Candidates

Internal candidates must be handled very carefully. If someone is qualified for the job, and you intend to offer it to the person, that is

---

great. However, if you have several employees who are qualified for the job and you only have one job vacancy, you must explain to each candidate the specific qualifications you're looking for and how you plan to make your selection. You never want the employees who didn't get the job to gang up on the employee who did and give her a hard time.

Again, make sure you have a good job description to give to anyone who's interested so she can determine if she is qualified. A good job description should focus on educational requirements, work experience, special skills, responsibilities, and job objectives such as sales quotas. It should also include the compensation range. Write a description that accurately reflects what the person performing that job will be doing on a daily basis. Never inflate it to look like a description for a more senior position.

To assure that the hiring process is fair and objective for all candidates, involve your management team and human resource staff right from the start. Even if they will not be directly involved in the interviews, ask for their critique on all aspects of your recruiting campaign.

What If an Employee Is Not Qualified?

What do you do with an employee who wants the job, but who doesn't have the right qualifications? Show her the job description and the specific qualifications you're looking for. Point out any qualifications you believe she does not have and ask her if she agrees with your assess-

───────────────── **WARNING** ─────────────────

Hire an outside candidate who is less qualified than an internal candidate, and you could face legal action.

ment. Listen carefully to her response. Perhaps she has additional qualifications you are not aware of that would give you cause to reconsider your decision. If she still doesn't seem qualified, provide her with some ideas on what she can do to improve should the position become available in the future.

SUMMARY

Make sure you do the proper planning before beginning the interview process. Try also to make the interview as natural as possible. You are looking to reach some form of agreement. The more conversational

---

WARNING

Many employees think they're qualified for any job you offer. If they're not, explain why in order to avoid any hard feelings.

IS A CANDIDATE'S APPEARANCE IMPORTANT?

You bet it is! Michael Deader managed President Reagan's news conferences. Deaver had Reagan stand in front of the open doors of the East Room for press conferences because it made the president appear more lively and substantive. He told reporters, "The open door with the light coming across the halls makes a much better picture of the president." Margaret Mead once told President Carter, "It doesn't matter what you say. What's important is how you look." In the business world, the same rules apply. Is the boss seen as too cold and too far removed from the troops? If he's going to spend the day out in the plant, why not wear work clothes and a hard hat to set a positive body language image. Never underestimate the importance of personal appearance in your organization.

HOW TO

There are three key people who should be involved in writing a job description: the immediate manager, the department head, and the human resource specialist.

and unstructured the interview, the more likely it is that you'll be able to gather quality information about the candidate and make an informed decision.

6

HOW DO YOU QUALIFY CANDIDATES DURING AN INTERVIEW?

S EVERAL YEARS AGO, SENATOR EDWARD KENNEDY WAS TRYING TO capture the Democratic Party's presidential nomination. During an interview with newsman Roger Mudd, he was asked why he wanted to become the president of the United States. He couldn't answer the question. It wasn't that he came up with a poor answer; he simply couldn't find any words at all. It seemed as if either he didn't want to be president or was just going through the motions to satisfy his father, Joe Kennedy. The public response was, "If he can't make a better case for himself than this, why should we vote for him? He must not be any good!" Shortly after the interview, the Edward Kennedy campaign was disbanded.

Senator Kennedy had made the same blunder that people who apply for jobs make everyday. He was trying to get the job, but couldn't tell anybody why he wanted it. If a candidate can't demonstrate a sincere interest in your job opening and tell you distinctly why they're the right person for the position, then you are wasting your time.

SELL EVERY CANDIDATE

Try to sell every candidate on the job, your organization, and the company from the very beginning. If a person isn't about the job, you are going to get mediocre responses to your questions. Assessing a candidate's suitability for a job is an ongoing process. Always promote the dynamics of the job and you'll get enthusiastic responses to your questions. Reassure candidates that if they join your staff, they will be a valued member of your organization.

Invite the candidate to give his opinion about anything you discuss. For example, if he tells you he can easily blend into your organization, ask why. Ask if he has any reservations about the job or company. If he tells you he has no reservations, ask why not. Everybody has to have some reservations if they are honest.

HOW DO YOU DEAL WITH CONCERNS?

Outstanding candidates will usually register some concerns during the interview that you must address if you want to attract them into your organization. If they don't have any concerns, they are probably not interested in the job. You must establish a good rapport with each candidate if you want them to openly express their thoughts.

Build trust so that applicants feel safe revealing hidden anxieties regarding the job. For example, do they fully understand what will be expected of them on a daily basis and can they meet the performance expectations? Can they balance their work and personal commitments? Such questions will help you determine if a candidate has a good understanding of the realities of the job and if their concerns are legitimate. Answer all of their concerns as best as you can. Then ask the question "Did I answer your concern to your satisfaction?"

Uncovering Frustrations

We all get frustrated when things don't go the way we expect. Outstanding employees know how to control their frustrations, which is an attribute that you want to discover during the interview process. They will get frustrated, but will they quickly dismiss frustrations with events they have no control over? For example, a purchasing agent may get frustrated over high interest rates, which are making it difficult to buy equipment the company needs. However, she will get over it quickly because she knows there's nothing she can do to change the situation. The last thing you want is to hire an employee who is perpetually frustrated with things that she has no control over. To find out how a candidate can cope with frustration, ask her: "What was the most frustrating aspect of your last position?"

What Don't You Like about Your Current Job?

There is a basic assumption that you must take into consideration when you interview anyone who is already employed. There is something about his current job that he doesn't like. It is probably one of the major reasons why he is trying to find another job. This is not a problem unless his dissatisfaction is due to an issue he could bring along to your organization. Ask him the question: "If you could change one aspect of your current job, what would it be?" If he tells you they would like to fire his boss, and you subsequently discover he didn't like his previous two bosses either, you are probably interviewing a person who can't accept authority. Remove him from your prospect list, and move on to your next candidate.

What Are Your Job-Related Concerns?

You don't want to extend an offer to a candidate unless you believe that she is comfortable with all aspects of the job. Does she have the skills to perform the job? Are the location and working hours acceptable? Does she like your company, its industry, and you? Is the compensation package acceptable? To find out, start by asking the question "Do you have any concerns about this job?" During the interview, ask questions that are directly related to the job or company. Avoid asking personal or emotional questions that have nothing to do with the job.

Can They Handle Challenges?

It's almost as easy for someone to accept a job offer as it is for them to quit the same job. The last thing you want to happen is to spend countless hours interviewing people, hire your best candidate, and then have her quit because she couldn't rise to the challenges of the job. Your candidates can't know what most of the job challenges are unless you explain them clearly in the interview. Then ask: "If you get this job, what will be your biggest challenge?" Listen carefully to determine whether or not they can rise to the challenges of the job.

QUESTIONS FOR DIFFERENT LEVELS OF CANDIDATES

Structure your interviews around the levels of jobs you're trying to fill. The higher the job level, the more sophisticated the interview questions and process will be. Focus on company issues. Openly discuss the work environment. Ask questions that focus on the candidate's understanding of the job, the industry, your company's culture, and specific job-related responsibilities. Also, try to discover why a candidate left his previous job. If he is employed, find out why he is interested in leaving his current position.

Entry-Level Candidates

Encourage entry-level candidates to discuss their experiences in school or to share an accomplishment that has significant personal meaning. These accomplishments can come from school, volunteer work, internship programs, and part- or full-time jobs. Probe entry-level candidates with questions to see if they are motivated and enthusiast about learning on the job.

Mid-Level Candidates

Mid-level candidates have typically been employed for at least a year and have completed their formal education. Ask questions that will allow you to determine how productive they will be within your organization. Does the candidate show initiative to take charge of a job assignment and add to the growth of your organization? You are not necessarily looking for quantifiable answers. However, try to find some indication of the candidate's ability to contribute to your organization.

High-Level Candidates

High-level candidates include the people you hire to fill management and executive positions in your company. They could also include people who want to fill technical or sales positions. You want to determine the impact candidates have had on the bottom line in their current organizations. Do they have profit and loss responsibility? Do they have

---

HOW TO

How do you find out what a candidate is looking for? Ask, What are his job expectations? Ask a candidate which other companies he has talked to. Try to find out if they have been able to meet all of his job expectations so far.

---

an assigned quota to meet? Have they been able to cut costs? How was their success achieved? Ask them to give you specific examples that will indicate how they will perform in your organization.

ASK THE RIGHT QUALIFYING QUESTIONS

Ask questions that will help you qualify each candidate's qualifications. Study her résumé carefully to help determine the right questions to ask. Try to get at the core of her accomplishments that she hopefully covered in her résumé so that you can ask qualifying questions. If she talks about an accomplishment, but doesn't give you a specific example, ask her for one in the interview. Ask her for the details and steps she took to complete an accomplishment.

By asking the right questions, you can determine if a candidate is knowledgeable about current technologies you employ in your company. Does she belong to an industry association that emphasizes these technologies? Can she show you training certificates that support her technical competence? Can she answer technical questions that satisfy you or the technical members of your staff?

IN*sight*

Everybody can boast about his accomplishments. If you ask tough qualifying questions, you'll be able to separate the fluff from the facts.

Watch Out for Repeaters

Watch out for candidates who tend to remain at the same level of duty when they switch jobs. If you ask what they did when they went from Job A to Job B and they tell you "The same thing," then a bell should go off in your head! If you are looking for an outstanding employee who has learned and grown professionally while moving from job to job, the "same old stuff" candidate probably won't fit your needs. If someone has been doing the same thing year after year, chances are she likes that kind of work environment. If she tells you she want to try something different, ask her why she waited until now to change. Listen carefully to her answer.

WARNING

A candidate who has been working at the same job for several years is probably going to be reluctant to accept change.

Explain Why You're Asking

Explain to candidates why you're asking particularly complex questions. Otherwise, they may be distracted by wondering why you're asking. They may stop listening to you and become irritated. They might think you are cross-examining them or may feel anxious if your question seems to demand they provide you with information. You can eliminate these problems if you precede your question with "Let me ask you a question to make sure I understand what you just said." This keeps you from jumping to the wrong conclusion about what the person has said. Also show your interest in what your candidate's are communicating, which in turn causes them to listen more attentively to you.

Ask Comparative Questions

Comparative interview questions are those that you ask all the job candidates. They allow you to fairly and objectively compare candidates once you complete the first round of interviews. When you ask a comparative question, you will often get forced and rigid responses. Many candidates are reluctant to open up and reveal much about themselves at first. This is not usually the case with outstanding candidates however. They tend to want to talk and tell you exactly what they think.

Comparative questions are typically open-ended. For example, you might ask: "Why do you feel you're the best person for this job? What are your strengths? What are you weaknesses? What really motivates you? What makes you lose your motivation?"

TAKING NOTES

If you're not blessed with photographic memory, take notes during the course of every interview. It makes it a lot easier to compare qualified candidates after all of the talking is done. A candidate may ask if he may also take notes during the interview. This is a good indication that you are talking to someone who is interested in the job. Encourage him to take all the notes he wants.

Make sure you jot down key words or phrases that pertain to the job. Keep equal-opportunity employment laws in mind when you take notes. Anything you write down should become included in an employment file. Such information can be requested by federal or state agencies investigating the employment practices of your company. Avoid taking notes on any discussions you may have about political or religious preferences. If you jot down notes on the candidate's résumé, make sure you also have a clean copy to give to others who interview the candidate. You don't want your notes to bias anyone else.

——————————————— **WARNING** ———————————————

*Be spare in your note taking. A candidate may become guarded
if he thinks you're trying to record his every word.*

WHO DO YOU LIKE?

Make sure you record how comfortable you feel with each candidate when you are interviewing several people with similar backgrounds. Takes notes once you conclude an interview session. Why did you feel comfortable or uncomfortable with this candidate? Who do you think will best respond to your direction? Who will be the most productive? Which candidate exhibits the most enthusiasm and interest in you and your organization?

Are They Compatible?

Evaluate each candidate's interpersonal skills. Is her personality and temperament compatible with your organization? Will she fit into your corporation's culture? What type of work environment does she prefer? What about work style? Is she comfortable in stressful situations or does she prefer a relaxed environment?

WHO STANDS OUT?

Is there something about what one candidate has to offer that makes her stand out? Perhaps a key accomplishment in a previous job impressed you. Or maybe she has overcome difficult odds to complete a major project, or just demonstrates a high level of enthusiasm about where she wants to go.

INsight

Encourage and listen to candidate feedback
every chance you get.

PLAN OF ACTION

Put together a standard checklist for every candidate. This list should include communication skills, personal appearance, attitude, and other relevant characteristics.

AVOID PESSIMISTS

In Disney's classic movie *Cinderella*, little Gus the mouse said, "If you don't have anything nice to say, don't say anything at all." Gus was talking about pessimists who never have anything nice to say. They're negative about everything, including themselves, and believe in the worst scenarios of Murphy's Law: "Whatever is right will go wrong, and whatever is wrong will never be right!" They aren't inhibited about letting others know how they feel and use the word "no" any chance they get. "I've tried it and it won't work" is one of their classic responses.

Pessimists are not fun to be around and are experts at destroying even the most optimistic of personalities. If you determine during the course of an interview session that you're talking to a pessimist, try to end the session as quickly as possible. How can you tell if people are pessimists? One indication is if they are more negative than positive in

CAN PESSIMISTS SERVE A PURPOSE?

Pessimists can be an invaluable resource if you use their skills to your advantage. For example, suppose you have an idea you know will work if only you can identify all of the problems involved in implementing it. Try presenting your idea to a pessimist. He will quickly tell you everything that can go wrong with your idea. Listen carefully. You can always discount any problems that don't seem relevant, but chances are the pessimist will identify problems you hadn't thought of.

their conversations. For example, if someone tells you he doesn't like his current co-workers, and didn't like the ones before that, watch out.

Closing the Interview

How do you close an interview? Always do it on a positive note. If you're talking to a candidate that you know won't meet your job specifications, simply thank him for taking the time to meet with you. If you are closing out an interview with an outstanding candidate that you really like, find out if he is interested in the job. Ask them the question: "If I offered you this job today, would you take it?" Assure your outstanding candidates that they're right for the job even though you can't commit to an offer yet.

HOW DO YOU UNCOVER HIDDEN PROBLEMS?

F ACE IT. WHEN PEOPLE ARE LOOKING FOR JOBS, THEY GENERally have a problem. They're either out of work, need to make more money, or don't like some aspect of their current job. It's important that you try to find out why they are interested in your job. Will you be able to satisfy whatever it is they need if you hire them? If they're looking for more money, will the salary you offer meet their needs? Or, will they accept your offer but leave as soon as a better offer comes along?

USE QUESTIONS TO UNCOVER HIDDEN PROBLEMS

Questions are powerful qualifying tools, and yet some people are reluctant to use questions in evaluating job candidates. Perhaps people believe that by asking a question, they're displaying their ignorance. Or they may think one can only ask so many questions before irritating the other person. If you're not an assertive kind of person, it may be difficult for you to ask questions.

In spite of the perceived drawbacks of asking questions, it's the best way to uncover a candidate's hidden problems. It requires quick and organized thinking and keen listening capabilities to reap the benefits you'll get from asking carefully worded questions.

You might ask a candidate the question "Why do you want this position?" Answers like "I want this position because I know I can do a great job" won't cut it. A more appropriate answer might be "I want this position because it is the focus of my career and fulfils my ambition of having the opportunity to implement my ideas for our growing company. I've been training to do just that over the past two years, and I'm the best person qualified for this position. Here's why." The reason a candidate wants the position should be listed at the top of her résumé, followed by a bulleted list of accomplishments that support her qualifications.

Qualifying Questions to Ask

You must ask tough qualifying questions if you want to find an outstanding candidate. There is a human tendency to not ask the tough questions for fear they will offend a candidate. However, if you introduce the question properly, both you and the candidate will benefit. For example, if you say "Do you mind if I ask you some questions that may be tough to answer? My intent is to make sure you would be comfortable joining our organization." Outstanding candidates will give you favorable responses since they are not interested in talking about mundane subjects.

Contribution Questions

Will your candidate be able to make a significant contribution to your organization? Find out by asking the question: "Tell me about a contribution you have recently made in your current job?" An outstanding candidate should be able to give you a specific example. It could even be an accomplishment outside of work, such as helping others in a community service environment. If the accomplishment is work related, find out how it benefited the company.

INsight

Candidates' accomplishments must be specific and directly related to their efforts. For example, perhaps they contributed directly to cost reductions or increasing sales.

Performance Questions

Is your candidate a performer who consistently delivers more than is expected and does so on time? Ask candidates the question "Have you ever delivered more than what was expected of you?" A "No" answer is not acceptable. Outstanding employees always deliver more than what is expected of them. You are looking for candidates to describe how they were able to enhance and add value to an important project. Ask what motivated them to push ahead and deliver more than the minimum requirement? Was this a one-time situation, or are they always motivated to achieve more than what is expected?

Compatibility Questions

Does your candidate relate well to others? Is he seen as a leader among his peers? To find out, ask the question: "If there was a problem at work, what would your colleagues ask you to do?" You want to find out if your candidate is a leader within his organization. You are looking for an example of how he helped resolve an awkward situation. Perhaps he interceded in a human resource problem with an employee or was instrumental in pulling together a team to resolve a major issue. Why did his teammates turn to him for help?

Are They Creative?

Creativity comes in a number of sizes and flavors. Can your candidate describe something he has done that was truly creative? It doesn't necessarily have to be a major project or effort. If you find him scratching his head, then you probably have the answer to your question. You want to determine if his way of thinking will fit into the creative process of your organization.

A creative person can usually come up with ways to quickly solve problems. They may also have innovative ideas, perhaps how to save money or develop new products or services. How do you find out if your candidate is creative? Ask him the question: "What is the most creative idea you've ever had?" As you evaluate candidates for more senior, leadership positions, it becomes more difficult to weigh factors that are critical to the job such as creativity and leadership skills. Many people can perform well in a structured organization without a lot of creativity or leadership skills. But if you're running a highly dynamic and entrepreneurial organization, these skills are critical to the overall success of the company.

Can They Solve Problems?

All organizations encounter problems every day of the week. Outstanding employees are able to decipher and come up with acceptable solutions to these problems on a routine basis. How can you determine if the candidate you're interviewing knows how to solve problems? Ask her the question "Have you recently discovered any significant problems at work, and how did you solve them?" You really want to determine if the candidate can think creatively under pressure.

What did she do to eliminate obstacles that were hindering a project or a task? Was her solution innovative?

Do They Have Good Perception?

An outstanding candidate knows how to look at and analyze a current situation, evaluate future trends, and decide what needs to be done. This quality can be invaluable to any organization. How do you find out if people have good perception? Ask them the question "Why do you think some companies with good products fail?" This question tests the candidates' abilities to analyze a company's strengths and weaknesses relative to its market strategy. Are they able to critically evaluate a situation and recommend appropriate solutions?

Do They Have Initiative?

You never want to hire someone, then find out later that the person likes to sit back and watch everybody else do the really tough jobs. You'll never catch this type of person volunteering for anything. You want a candidate who is willing to dive into a bad situation and make it better, or better yet, take charge of and improve an already good situation. Outstanding candidates like exciting challenges and are not afraid of change. How do you find out if they have any initiative? Ask them the question "Describe to me an improvement that you initiated. Why was it important to your company?"

Can They Influence Others?

Lots of people have great ideas. The key is being able to sell their ideas to others. How can you tell if candidates know how? Ask the question "Have you ever had to persuade others to adopt your idea? If so, what was your idea and how did you sell it?" Does it sound as if the candidate was sensitive to other people's issues and concerns? Was there resistance to the idea, and if so, how was it overcome? These questions are testing the candidate's communication skills and ability to persuade others.

Will They Be Honest with You?

Honesty is never an option. Employees who lie to you about their work is a major problem. How can you tell if your candidates will be honest and candid? Ask them to describe one of their projects that failed. Beware if they tell you they have never had a failed project. They have either never had a project assigned to them or they are not telling you the truth. You want to determine how your candidates handle failure. Do they learn from their mistakes? Are they afraid of failing? People who are afraid of failing have difficulty making decisions and may lie to cover their tracks.

INsight

The person who never makes a decision
will never make a mistake.

DO THEY HAVE THE SKILLS THAT YOU NEED?

Try to determine if a candidates have the basic skills you need early in the selection process. If you don't see these skills in their résumés, or learn about them in an initial telephone interview, those candidates are probably not on your "face-to-face" interview list. Even the candidates on your interview list who appear to have the skills you need may differ significantly in their ability to perform. Probe candidates with questions that will uncover their ability to perform specific aspects of the job.

Ask your candidates to elaborate on the skills that make them unique and attractive. Can they illustrate how these skills will be beneficial in the job you're trying to fill? If a candidate cites only standard skills that meet the minimum job requirements, then you are probably not talking to a potentially outstanding employee.

What Are Their Strengths?

What are your candidates' strong points? Watch out if they hesitate in answering this question. Outstanding candidates know their strong points. Are they introspective enough to relate these strengths to your job requirements? This will show that they not only understand the job requirements, but also know how to apply their strengths to meet any challenge.

What Are Their Weaknesses?

What are your candidates' weak points? Outstanding candidates will honestly tell you how they can improve to bring more value to your organization. If they respond with "I have no weaknesses," they are either naïve or immature and probably don't belong on your list of active candidates. A good follow-up question for those who have just divulged their weak points is "What can you do to minimize or eliminate your weak points?" Do the candidates have a self-improvement plan in place?

WARNING

Beware of "canned" responses such as "I work too hard" or "I am too much of a perfectionist" when you ask a candidate about weaknesses. Many people will rehearse an answer to this question to make it sound positive.

Do They Have Experience?

Find out if candidates have experience you need by asking the question "How is your experience relevant to this job?" You want to find out if they know which of their skills fit the job you're trying to fill. Can they clearly describe the skills the job requires? It will be difficult for candidates to answer this question if you haven't given them a chance to review the job description and briefed them on the specific functions of the job. Be sure to give them this information before asking the question.

THE JOB CHANGER

Ask any potentially outstanding candidate with a history of job changes the following question "Why have you changed jobs so frequently?" It's important that you know the reason for each job change. Was it due to an external force, like a layoff that was outside the candidate's control? Or was the problem internal? Be sure you feel comfortable with the candidate's response.

WATCH FOR BODY LANGUAGE AND APPEARANCE PROBLEMS

People communicate messages not only through words, but also through body language. Body language is the looks and moves you make with various parts of your body either to reinforce and strengthen or to contradict what you are saying. You can learn a lot about your interviewees by watching their body language and observing their personal appearance.

Hundreds of books have been written about communicating with body language. Some people spend their entire lives studying the effects of body language in the workplace and showing others how to interpret it. It's not hard to learn to use body language effectively. But, you don't just reach out, grab it, and call yourself an expert. You have to learn it the old fashion way, a little bit at a time.

Foot Language

The bottom of the foot is a sensitive part of the body. Most people will expose the soles of their shoes only when they feel they are in a protected position and are comfortable. Watch what candidates do with their feet. They are displaying a sense of self-assurance and control if they're sitting back, one leg crossed over the other. The moment discussions turn serious and the people are challenged with tough questions, they may suddenly uncross their legs, lean forward, and place both feet firmly on the ground. This indicates that they are nervous and uncomfortable about giving you an honest answer to your question. Furthermore, if you see people suddenly pull their feet back under their chair, they are probably afraid or concerned about something that was just said.

Swing Language

A candidate may show impatience or doubt by swinging her feet back and forth. For example, if you ask a candidate if she plans to stay with your organization for a reasonable period of time and she starts swinging her feet, you have your answer. Move on to your next candidate.

Protective Body Language

You may occasionally interview a candidate in his office. Perhaps it's an internal candidate, or going to the person's workplace is more convenient. Analyzing a candidate's desk can help you determine his personal style. An insecure person will often sit behind a huge wooden desk that acts as a barricade. Try to tempt the person to move out from behind his fortress to a sofa or chair in an open area.

One way to do this is to ask the candidate to join you for lunch or coffee in the cafeteria. If this doesn't work, put your briefcase on the desk before you start talking.

This will infringe on the person's protective space and probably make him nervous. The idea is to disrupt his secure position, which he will maintain as long as he is sitting behind his fortress. A person is more prone to give you guarded answers to your question in this position. It may be appropriate to move on to your next candidate if you can't get the person to move.

PERSONAL APPEARANCE

My friend Bill Mitchell is a classic example of how one's appearance can destroy job opportunities. Mitchell was the chief financial officer (CFO) for one of Phillip Morris's subsidiary companies in California. He has an MBA in finance from Columbia University and is highly qualified to be any company's CFO. Because the subsidiary company didn't fit into Philip Morris's line of business, it was sold off, and Mitchell was replaced by the acquiring company's CFO. In other words, Bill was out of a job.

Mitchell came to me for advice on how to mount an executive search campaign. I told him, "Bill, you have to shave your beard and mustache off if you want to improve your CFO image. Like it or not, finance executives typically have very conservative tastes." Mitchell quickly discounted my comment and told me "If they won't accept me the way I look, the hell with them."

I empathized with Mitchell's comment and tried to convince him that he could always grow his beard back after he landed a position. However, he was still bent on ignoring job appearance. A year later, Mitchell was still looking for a job and in fact, hadn't even gotten an offer. Fortunately, he had saved enough money to buy a small business, keep his beard, and run it the way he saw fit. However, the point is that other companies know that appearance is important.

There are some legal issues surrounding personal appearance that dictate what you can and cannot do after you have hired an employee. But, you can consider personal appearance before hiring an employee. Some people would take issue with that statement, but that's the way it is.

If appearance is an important factor in the job you're trying to fill and a candidate doesn't meet your requirements, move on to the next candidate. It's very difficult, if not impossible, to get someone to change their appearance to accommodate work standards after you hire them. Trying to do so could present all kinds of problems.

ALWAYS GET A SECOND OPINION

Just when you think you have been doing pretty well at hiring people, you make a big mistake and hire the wrong person. You realize you should have known better. This can happen to anyone. Hiring is a subjective process that is based on lots of soft information and your intuition. Try to have at least one other person interview your final candidates. A third party's fresh perspective may surprise you.

SUMMARY

How do you uncover hidden problems? Everybody has at least one problem and candidates who tells you they don't should be scratched from your list. If they lie to you in an interview, they'll lie a lot more when they are working for you. Don't be afraid to ask the suggested tough qualifying questions. It's the only way you're going to find out about a candidate's specific problems and know whether those problems would prove to be disruptive to your organization. Several suggestions in this chapter, including the perspective on personal appearance, are legally controversial. However, you can't ignore these issues if you want to develop an outstanding organization.

WARNING

*Get written permission from a candidate before you conduct
any background checks. This way you will be
sure what you do is legal.*

HOW DO YOU SELL A CANDIDATE ON YOUR ORGANIZATION?

T HE POWERFUL ART OF PERSUADING CANDIDATES TO JOIN YOUR organization is critical to the recruiting process. The more you sell the benefits about your organization, the more candidates will be interested in joining you. Always stress benefits and opportunities you offer throughout an interview. Suppose you say to a candidate "I need someone like you to take over the Harding project." The project is the opportunity you want to sell.

You must also offer the benefit part of the equation. So, you add "It will be a tough challenge but if you are successful, it could catapult your career onto the fast-track in our organization." Think about all of the benefits you can bring to the table, and then suggest them in order of importance whenever the opportunity presents itself.

MASTERING THE ART OF PERSUASION

Have you ever caught yourself saying "That potentially outstanding employee doesn't know what I'm trying to tell him. How am I ever going to get to him accept my offer?" You can solve the problem by becoming an effective and persuasive communicator. This is a skill you must learn to master if you want to hire top-notch people.

Persuasion versus Manipulation

First, it is important to understand the difference between persuasion and manipulation. Many people think that persuasion is just a kinder word for manipulation. However, there's a huge difference between the two terms.

According to *Webster's Dictionary*, manipulation is the act of using any means necessary to force a person to do something that fulfills your needs, whether or not it's in their best interest. Persuasion is the art of guiding someone through a logical progression of thoughts so that they can arrive at a conclusion that compliments your views and is also in their own best interest. Persuasion enables the other person to understand what you are saying and what you are feeling, and motivates them to do what you believe is in their best interest.

How Persuasion Works

A classic example of persuasion occurred when I was in Army boot camp. I was talking to my buddy while one of the sergeants was conducting a class on how to avoid explosive land mines. The sergeant interrupted our conversation and said "You better listen to what I'm telling you, boy, because it could save your life." From then on, I was all ears. He had told me why I should listen and persuaded me to do so.

In the business-recruiting world, you're constantly challenged to get candidates to listen to what you have to say. Don't assume all candidates will listen to you just because you're the one offering the job.

Outstanding candidates typically have several job opportunities they are considering. They will shut you out and move on to the next job opportunity unless you capture their imagination.

USING HOOKS

What allures, entices, captivates, and tantalizes someone? It's a hook. A hook is a statement used specifically to get attention. Hooks are dangled in front of you every hour of the day and night as you watch television, listen to the radio, and read newspapers and magazines. Newspaper hooks are called headlines. Television and radio stations call their hooks teasers. Do you remember the hook in Burger King's classic television commercial that showed a little old lady eating a competitor's hamburger and asking "Where's the beef?" What a great hook! There are three basic types of hooks. Try using them during interviews.

THE HOOK

A hook can be a statement or an object. Using a hook is an excellent way to get your audience's attention during a presentation. A hook statement should be no more than 30 seconds.

Personal Hook

The personal hook is one of the most effective hooks you can use. The sergeant used my life as a personal hook to persuade me to listen. Name-dropping can be another effective personal hook. Suppose you're interviewing an outstanding candidate who you want to hire. You'd give anything to have this person on your team. How can you personally hook this candidate? You ask the question "Tomorrow, I am having dinner with our CEO. Would you and your spouse like to join us?" This statement uses two personal hooks to influence a candidate's decision: the offer to meet the company's CEO and a free dinner.

Persuasive Hook

The persuasive hook uses effective questions to get a candidate's attention. The question should be very specific. You want the candidate to think carefully before she responds. You also want to get information you can use to persuade her to do something.

Say you have a great idea on how to promote a new product. The candidate that you are interviewing has the expertise to help make it happen. Somehow, you need to persuade her to accept and get excited about your ideas. You have told her about your idea and how it fits into the job. Now ask the question "What do you think about the new product we're about to introduce?"

The question gets the candidate to focus her thoughts on the new product and opens the door for you to discuss your product introduction ideas. Her response should provide valuable information to help you determine if she's qualified for the job. Suppose she says, "It's a great product but quite frankly, I'm having a tough time figuring out how you're going to introduce it." You just hit pay dirt. You're talking to a potentially outstanding candidate who knows how to think. Follow up with questions on why she feels it will be difficult to introduce the product.

Strong-Statement Hooks

The third persuasive hook uses a strong statement. Here's an example. You walk into your office for a second meeting with an outstanding candidate, shut the door, and abruptly say, "If we don't take some immediate action, we're going to lose our largest account. Do you have any ideas that will prevent that from happening?" This hook statement will capture your candidate's immediate attention and get him to focus on the problem. Don't expect him to have a solution for a problem that he

---

HOW TO

Use the personal, persuasive, and strong-statement hooks as powerful tools to persuade outstanding candidates to join your organization.

---

knows little or nothing about. But an outstanding candidate will ask meaningful questions and demonstrate his ability to critically analyze problems. Your effective use of strong-statement hooks will get your candidate to focus on a specific subject.

JANE FONDA HOOKED HER AUDIENCES

Jane Fonda used personal, persuasive, and strong-statement hooks in her fitness video commercials. "Hi, I'm Jane Fonda and I have an important message for you (personal hook). Are you one of the 50 million Americans who try to lose weight each year (persuasive hook)? Diets simply don't work as you'll learn when you order my tape (strong statement hook). This 15-second commercial persuaded millions of people to run out and buy Jane's fitness video.

THE FINAL PERSUADER

There's one final persuasive technique you can use to sell a candidate on a job. Show what he will gain. Every person has a desire for gain and if he perceives that he will gain by following your persuasive lines of thought, he'll take action. Jane Fonda offered listeners a free copy of her fitness book if they ordered her video within a specified time frame. This is an example of a materials-goods gain. Personal gain can include security, acceptance, success, and wealth.

SUMMARY

Try to use all three hooks in your interview. Make sure everything you say treats your candidate with respect. Avoid making any condescending remarks. Identify all the benefits your organization offers and show how they fulfill the candidate's needs. Focus on a person's two greatest motivating factors, the desire for gain and the fear of loss. List every possible objection the candidate could have to joining your organization. Then determine how you will overcome each of these objections.

INsight

Continue to sell the candidate on the job, company, and geographic location as you gather information about him.

GET TO KNOW YOUR CANDIDATE

Offer your top candidate an opportunity to spend a day with your team to hedge your bet. Take him or her out to dinner for a "compatible fit" test. Make introductions to the key players in your organization. Invite the candidate to talk to key customers and suppliers for testimonials.

Close the sales part of an interview by assuring your candidate that he is right for the job. Tell him that even though you can't commit to an offer at this time, he is on the top of your list. Tell him when you will make your final decision and when you will contact him. Find out if he is interested in the job by asking "If I were able to offer this job to you right now, would you take it?"

WHAT IF THE CANDIDATE REJECTS YOUR OFFER?

B E SURE YOU KNOW A CANDIDATE'S SALARY, BENEFITS, AND CAREER expectations before extending her an offer. Is the candidate looking for a bonus that is beyond your company's means? The candidate's idea of a commission plan for a sales position may be completely different than yours. Can you meet her expectations? Make sure you address all of these issues before making an offer.

A candidate will usually reject your offer if you can't meet most of her expectations. All you can do is accept her rejection if it's for reasons beyond your control. However, if it's for a reason that you can address, then start negotiating. Be sure to find out precisely why she rejected your initial offer.

THE OFFER LETTER

Dear Ms. Doe:

I hereby offer you the position of full-time Senior Project Manager at XYZ Corporation. Your first date of employment will be xx/xx/xx. Your compensation will be $$, payable every two weeks, which is equivalent to a $$ annual salary. Your first salary review will take place on or before xx/xx/xx.

Your first 90 days of employment will be an initial employment period. Upon successful completion of this probationary period, you will be eligible for sick leave, which accrues at the rate of one day per month, and the company's medical insurance, life insurance, disability insurance, and 401k plans. This offer will remain in effect until xx/xx/xx. Please notify us at your earliest convenience if you accept the offer as stated.

WHY DID THE CANDIDATE TURN YOU DOWN?

When a candidate rejects an offer, try to find out why. This is one of the most difficult recruiting tactics to apply; however it can offer the biggest payback. There is a tendency to jump into a conversation and respond to an objection just to get it out of the way. But a candidate who has just turned down your job offer may not be listening to you. He is thinking about what else he can say to buttress his objection.

Link the Candidate's Thinking with Yours

Ask the candidate a question about his objection. This will help you understand exactly why they made it and link his thinking to yours. You want to know his reasoning. Suppose you're trying to convince someone to join your organization and help install a new time-saving machine. If he replies "That's too complicated," how can you

---

INsight

Questions are powerful and versatile interview tools.
Use them whenever you can.

---

counter his objection if you don't know what he means by complicated? Don't forget, by inquiring into an objection, you're showing interest in the candidate's concerns.

Diagnosing Objections

It's important to reduce a candidate's natural resistance to a career change when you're trying to get him to join your organization. You respond to his objection, but only after you understand his line of reasoning. His objection shows that his thinking is not in line with yours. You must diagnose what caused the problem before you can render a solution. Ask questions to learn the person's reasoning before you respond.

Diagnosing Loose Objections

Loose objections are based on either questionable facts or no facts. This makes them difficult to diagnose. Suppose your candidate tells you he doesn't want the job because someone he knows says your

---

WARNING

Candidates who throw out loose objections may simply be looking for an excuse to turn a job down. Don't waste your time with these people. An outstanding candidate isn't afraid to tell you exactly why they turned a job down.

---

organization isn't going anywhere. Start asking questions that will get him to reason with you:"Has the person ever worked for my company? What expertise does this individual have to be able to draw this conclusion? Did the person give you specifics to support the opinion that my company isn't going anywhere.?"Once you find the weak points that are inherent in the objection, you can show why the objection is not valid.

LEAD WITH YOUR BEST FOOT FORWARD

Lead with an offer that is both fair and reasonable. Underpay someone and she may bolt as soon as she gets a better offer. But overpay someone and you'll upset the salary scale in your organization. You should have a pretty good idea of what it will take to attract a candidate if you've asked the right questions in the interview.

--- WARNING ---

If you overpay a new employee thinking no one else will find out, beware. Everyone will know.

What If a Candidate Rejects Your Salary Offer?

You've just made an offer to your top candidate when she tells you, "Although I like your company and the job sounds great, I can't make it on the salary you're offering."What do you do? First find out what her salary expectations are to see if you're both on the same playing field. Ask the question "What compensation were you expecting?" Notice the use of the word "compensation" instead of "salary."

Salary implies a dollar amount posted on a paycheck. Compensation covers not only a person's salary, but other monetary benefits as well. For example, suppose your candidate wants $5,000 more than your offer. You learned in the interview that she wants to continue her college education. Your company has a $6,000 per year tuition reimbursement program that's not offered by her current employer. That's your potential salary-compensation bridge.

Your counterresponse might go something like this: "I think we can meet all of you compensation requirements when you consider our $6,000 a year education benefit. You can apply it to the school of your choice and it's tax-free. Do we have a deal?" If the candidate continues to request a salary that's beyond your means, politely dismiss her and proceed on to your next choice.

PLAN OF ACTION

Always find out why a candidate rejects a salary offer. It could help you determine the appropriate salary level for the job.

The Candidate Rejects the Job's Location

Sometimes a candidate will reject your offer because she doesn't want to live in the town or city where the job is located. Dealing with this problem can be more challenging than meeting a candidate's salary demands. Anyone required to live in an area she doesn't like will probably start looking for a job in a more preferred area as soon as she accepts your offer.

Find out what she doesn't like about the job's location to determine if you can address her concerns. Ask the question "What is it about the location that you don't like?" Perhaps she tells you she heard the school system is terrible. If you have solid information that shows otherwise, you may be able to convince her that the job's location will meet or exceed her expectations. If she tells you she doesn't like the

> ### PLAN OF ACTION
>
> Don't hide the facts if location is a determining factor in the job you're trying to fill. Be sure everyone you interview knows about the job location even before you meet.

winter climate, then you're stuck unless you can convince her that shoveling snow is a great way to exercise.

The Candidate Rejects Your Benefit Program

You've asked your outstanding candidate if he accepts your offer and he tells you "I like everything you have to offer but to be frank, your benefits program is sadly inadequate." Suppose you're running a start-up company and know intuitively your benefits program lags behind the competition. How do you deal with this kind of objection? Here's where you have to put your sales hat on.

Find out what the candidate doesn't like about your benefits program. It's best to address the issue directly even if you know your benefit program leaves something to be desired. Your counterstatement might go something like this: "You're right. Our benefits program needs to be upgraded and we're working on doing just that. However, have you considered the added advantages of joining a fast-growing start-up company? In the next two years we plan to double in size and have a benefits program that far exceeds anything our competition can offer. You will also find more advancement opportunities here than anywhere else. Would you like to reconsider and join our company?"

The Candidate Doesn't Like the Job

What do you do if the candidate says "I don't want the job because it is not what I expected." It's tough to turn around that kind of a rejection and maybe you should not even try. Why did this person apply for the job and now say he doesn't want it? Perhaps you misrepresented the job in your ad campaign or during the interview discussions. You have to ask the question "What is it about this job that you don't like?" You want to know if your candidate understands the job requirements. Perhaps he misunderstood some specific aspect of the job that you can address.

PLAN OF ACTION

If a candidate rejects your offer because he doesn't like the job, make sure you give him a copy of the job description. Ask him to read it and determine if it clarifies any of his concerns.

SUMMARY

There are several methods to persuade outstanding candidates to reconsider an initial rejection of your job offer. However, it is not wise to try to convince someone to accept the job if the stated reasons for rejecting it show that the person would not fit into your organization. If the job was rejected because of misinformation, then it is appropriate to clarify the issues and resubmit your offer. Always remember to send a thank you letter to every candidate who rejects your offer. You never know when your paths may cross again.

Ask every candidate who rejects your offer if he knows anyone else who might be interested in the job. He may know someone who would be well qualified for the job. If he doesn't volunteer the information, ask him directly if he knows of someone right for the position. It never hurts to ask.

10

WHY SHOULD YOU ONLY HIRE TEAM LEADERS?

*T*HE *WALL STREET JOURNAL* RECENTLY PUBLISHED AN ARTICLE BY United Technology Corporation. It read, "People don't want to be managed, they want to be led. Whoever heard of a world manager? They're called world leader, right? Educational leader. Political leader. Religious leader. Scout leader. Community leader. Labor leader. Business leader. They all lead. They don't manage. The carrot always wins over the stick. Ask your horse. You can lead a horse to water, but you can't manage him to drink."

Effective teaming has become a critical component of nearly every modern organization. Your ability to find and hire team leaders is critical to the success of your organization. People can have outstanding credentials and work for team-oriented companies, but not be good team leaders.

Never consider a candidate who you don't believe will be an outstanding team leader.

IN*sight*

Manage yourself before you try to manage someone else. Do that well
and you'll be ready to stop managing and start leading.

WHAT ALL TEAMS NEED

All teams need team leaders. They don't need team managers. Your organization will succeed if you hire people who have the ability to become outstanding team leaders. What is the difference between a manager and a leader? A manager administers, maintains, and plans. A leader innovates, develops, and sets direction. This is not to say that a person cannot be both a strong manager and a good leader. That's what you want. Harvard business professor John Kotter said: "Most U.S. companies are still overmanaged and underled today. However, with careful selection, nurturing, and encouragement, dozens of people can play important leadership roles in a business organization." Here are eight leadership traits you should look for in potential employees:

Hire People Who Have Vision

Outstanding team leaders are able to develop a vision, a mental image of where they want the team to go that's in the best interest of the organization. This vision must be effectively communicated to every member of their teams to assure that everybody is on the same page. But, it is also a two-way street. Leaders must also have a personal vision for their own desires that compliments the goals and objectives of your organization.

Hire People with Scope

Effective team leaders are able to see the big picture of the team's mission. They understand both the short and long-term ramifications if the team doesn't accomplish its mission. Good leaders know how to work with all the members of a team, including helping the weaker members to assure the success of the overall team.

INsight

Harvey Mackay, the author of numerous books on leadership, once said,
"It doesn't matter how well you're leading if no one's following."

Hire People with Innovative Ideas

Great team leaders are not afraid to step out on the leading edge and make innovative decisions. Teams are often formed to develop innovative ideas and thinking.

Outstanding team leaders know how to excite their team members with innovative ideas and how to lead them to implement those ideas.

Hire People with Focus

A team will often lose focus on what it is chartered to accomplish. Good team leaders remain focused on the team's mission. They know how to identify their major objectives and are not diverted by minor issues. They help control the direction of the team rather than allowing something else to control it for them.

Hire Rational People

Who can forget the closing minutes of the 1978 Gator Bowl when Woody Hayes, one of the top coaches in the country, ran onto the field and punched a player who had just made a key interception? Ohio

State fired him the next day. People who can't control their emotions should not be team leaders. Confrontations are common in a team setting. They can open up communication channels for healthy dialogue as long as they are controlled. Rational team leaders know how to control confrontations so that they don't erupt into damaging personal encounters.

Hire People Who Can Deal with Pressure

Forming a team to tackle critical problems and issues invites pressure. The pressure can take many forms, including tight deadlines, working long hours, and accommodating the multiple personalities of different team players. Good team leaders know how to handle pressure. They know how to recognize a pressure situation and how to control their emotions. They're also experts at introducing thoughts and ideas that relieve the pressure on other team members.

Hire People Who Can Teach

Team leaders give to others by teaching themeverything they know. This is important in a team environment and assures that everybody is operating at approximately the same level. A typical team will have players with varying degrees of knowledge. Outstanding team leaders recognize when certain players need help and quickly teach them what they need to know.

Hire People Who Involve Others

All members of an effective team need to be 100 percent involved. However, people have different personality types. Some like to be involved. Other want to be involved, but because of their personality will quietly sit back and say nothing. A good leader knows how to coax the quieter members to participate in team discussions. They encourage all team members to present their opinions and ideas.

MAKE A GREAT FIRST IMPRESSION

You must be an outstanding team leader yourself if you want to attract others. You must therefore create a great first impression with every candidate you interview. You never get a second chance to make a good first impression. You can succeed or fail in first impressions every day in briefings, interviews, phone calls, and meetings. In today's fast-paced work environment, deals are won or lost, careers are made or destroyed, and relationships are established or broken all in a matter of minutes based upon first impressions.

HOW TO

How do you become a team leader? Not just by saying you are one. You become a leader through what you do, not what you say.

The Research

Research shows that lasting impressions are formed in four minutes or less. After this, it becomes much more difficult, if not impossible, to sell, persuade, or influence anyone to join your organization. Those first four minutes can make or break your recruiting efforts. According to the psychology community, over 90 percent of the impressions we make have nothing to do with what we say. More than half are based on how we look. Most of the rest depend on how we sound. Only a small percentage depend on our verbal message.

First Impressions Are Critical

First impressions are often based on the things people notice about you in the first three or four minutes they meet you. Your appearance, facial expressions, movements, tone of voice, and words all help someone form a first impression of you. You can generally count on a candidate's interest in your organization if you've made a positive first impression.

COMMUNICATIONS SKILLS ARE CRITICAL

You may not realize how many first impressions you make in a day. You spend 85 percent of your day in some form of communication (i.e., speaking, listening, or writing). The typical worker makes 10 to 12 speeches per year to staff, peers, superiors, community groups, and professional associations. Most people spend more time on the telephone than they do on their personal computers. According to *Harvard Business Review*, communication skills rate second only to job knowledge as an important factor in a person becoming a successful leader.

SUMMARY

The quality of team leadership in any business is directly related to its success. Some people are natural leaders. Others must learn to lead. Anyone can grow into being a leader if the seeds of experience, imagination, and innovation take root. As Notre Dame coach Vince Lombardi once said, "The strength of a team is in the strength of its leader." Look for leadership attributes in any employee you hire.

WHAT CAN YOU DO TO MINIMIZE EMPLOYEE TURNOVER?

F ACE IT. IT TAKES A LOT OF TIME AND MONEY TO FIND, RECRUIT, and hire an outstanding employee. The last thing you want is to hire someone, then immediately watch them find another job opportunity. Be skeptical whenever you're interviewing a frequent job changer. Your outstanding candidate probably had several job offers before she accepted yours and knows she is a marketable commodity.

WHAT TO WATCH OUT FOR

Outstanding people working for other companies are often receptive to outside job offers. People have a natural tendency to better themselves, particularly if they can do it with the security of stability and strength. There are also many outstanding candidates who are risk takers. Some particularly

TAKE NOTHING FOR GRANTED

Never take it for granted that your best will stay with you forever. Always reinforce their personal value and the opportunities and benefits of their long-term relationship with your organization. As soon as you begin taking employees for granted, you open the door for your competitors to steal them.

aggressive candidates want to ultimately go into business for themselves. So think carefully before trying to recruit an independent entrepreneurial maverick. You don't want to hire people whose priorities are to use your paychecks to build their nest eggs and fund their own ventures.

To keep good people, you must attract the right ones in the first place. Everything you do to make your company more appealing to outsiders will also benefit those already on your team. Your recruiting effort will be more successful if you create an image that your employees are choice assets.

PLAN OF ACTION

Do you believe that you are talking to a frequent job hopper? You may want to cut her from your active list, regardless of how good she sounds.

QUESTIONS YOU MUST ASK TO UNCOVER TURNOVER PROBLEMS

Be sure to prepare several tough qualifying questions for anyone you believe is a frequent job changer. Outstanding candidates know they are hot commodities in the job market. Consider the answers you would like to get to each question you ask. What kinds of answers don't you want to get? Focus your attention on one important question: "If I hire

---

WARNING

---

*Most frequent job changers are well versed in answering questions
on why they have a short job tenure history. Watch out for
perfectly rehearsed responses to your questions.*

---

this candidate, will he stay with my organization for a reasonable period of time?"

Why Do You Want to Leave Your Current Job?

The "canned" answer that you may get when you ask why someone
wants to leave his current job may sound something like this: "I've gone
as far as I can go in my current job. I've learned everything there is to
know about the position and unless someone leaves, I will never get
promoted." You need to counter with a qualifying question: "What makes
you believe that this job with my organization will be any different than
your current job?" Listen very carefully to his answer. It better have substance. If he tells you it's because you have a dynamic organization and
he thinks you are great, watch out. But, if he identifies specific aspects
of the job that would be challenging, then it may be worth your while
to go on to the next qualifying question.

What Are You Looking for in Your Next Job?

Your candidate's answer to this question will help you determine
whether or not you can meet his short and long-term expectations.
The "canned" answer you may get goes something like this: "I'm looking for a challenging job in a growing and dynamic organization."
Again, you need to ask him exactly what he is looking for. The words
"challenging" and "growing" don't tell you anything. Ask him the question "What do you find challenging about the job I may offer?" Can the

candidate demonstrate he truly understands some of the challenges of the job?

Your follow-up question should be "Why do you think our organization is growing?" Has the candidate done some research on your organization before the interview? A nebulous response like "I just know you're a great company" probably indicates you're interviewing someone who isn't serious about wanting to work for you. A serious candidate will be able to tell you why he thinks your company is great.

How Have Your Motivations Changed Over the Past Few Years?

Watch out for "same old...same old" responses like: "I have to be challenged." "Work has to be exciting for me." A worthy candidate should be able to demonstrate that she has learned and matured through her job changes. How will what she has learned make her a better employee in your organization? Move on to your next candidate if you're not satisfied with the person's answer.

IN*sight*

Remember that frequent job changers tend to be immature and have unrealistic expectations of what they are worth in the job market.

Why Is This Job Especially Suited to You?

If a candidate tells you it's because it's what she always wanted to do, ask her "Then why did you wait until now to do it?" An outstanding candidate should know what she wants to do and be able to tell you which areas of responsibilities in your position are attractive to her. Both her personality and skills should be compatible with the position. Is the candidate emotionally mature enough to handle the demands of the job? Ask her the question "What will keep you from leaving if the going gets tough?" Move on to your next candidate if all you get is a blank stare.

What Are Your Goals and Objectives Over the Next Five Years?

There are a couple of things to remember about goals. A goal must have an objective and a definite end date. A candidate who tells you their goal is to be happy for the rest of his life has no idea what goals are all about. An outstanding candidate is a person who has very specific goals and a well thought-out plan on how to achieve them. He should be able to tell you how your job opportunity fits into that plan. Outstanding candidates have a consistent focus and purpose in their career development plan.

Will You Stay with Us?

Don't be afraid to ask a candidate "If I hire you, will you stay with us for a reasonable period of time?" Does your candidate's answer show he has grown and developed as a person over the past couple of years? Is he ready to settle down and focus on long-term rather than short-term career objectives? Is he in control of his personal life and does it fit into his career objectives? Remember you are technically not allowed to ask personal questions during an interview. However, most candidates will divulge quite a lot of personal information anyway. Listen carefully to what they say about their personal lives. Anyone with an unstable personal life probably doesn't have a very stable professional life either.

Why Would You Quit?

Here's a great question to ask: "If I hired you and you quit, what would be the most likely reason?" This is one of the toughest questions you can ask a job changer. She may have trouble explaining if she is not ready to settle down in a job. Watch out for answers like: "Gee, this is what I have been looking for all along. I can't imagine why I would ever want to leave." An outstanding candidate must convince you that the only reason she would leave you would be for something that's unforeseen and unrelated to your company. No employer can prevent someone from changing her mind and leaving the organization. However, the hiring process is expensive and time consuming. You must be sure that you are hiring someone who will stay with you for a reasonable period of time.

————————————————— **WARNING** —————————————————

Watch out for candidates who cite salary as the most likely reason for changing jobs. They'll be on the lookout for a better paying position soon after you hire them.

Lessons Learned or Not Learned

Does your candidate learn from experience? Ask her the question: "What's the single most important thing you've learned in your career?" The perfect answer is "compatibility." A candidate who gives you a long-winded answer implying that they have difficulty working with others is not worth considering.

SUMMARY

One common thread binds all of these questions together. Look for an outstanding candidates who can describe the experience and knowledge they have gained in their different jobs. Are they now ready to settle down and join an organization for the long-term?

Many of the suggested questions are deliberately tough questions. They are designed to help you pin down and qualify potential job hoppers. Certainly, good job hoppers can give you fake and well-rehearsed answers. But, watch their body language. Are they twitching when they answer your questions? Do they look you directly in the eye when they answer? Do their answers sound rehearsed? You can almost always tell when someone is not giving you an honest answer.

12

HOW DO INFORMAL REWARDS HELP RETAIN OUTSTANDING EMPLOYEES?

S OME OF THE MOST EFFECTIVE FORMS OF RECOGNITION COST nothing. A sincere word of thanks from the right person at the right time can mean more to an employee than a raise, a formal reward, or a fancy plaque. Part of the power of informal rewards comes from the knowledge that someone took the time to notice the achievement, seek out the person responsible, and deliver praise.

Informal rewards are spontaneous and include forms of recognition that can be implemented with minimal planning and effort. In a recent study at Wichita State University, Dr. Gerald Graham stressed that the most powerful motivator for an employee is a manager's personalized and instant recognition. Graham adds, "simply asking an employee to get involved in a situation is motivational in itself."

EASY WAYS TO IMPLEMENT INFORMAL REWARDS

Informal rewards are often more effective and less expensive than formal ones. Studies show that managers who actively use informal rewards to motivate their employees elicit the highest job satisfaction and performance. Informal rewards are usually easy to implement and should be an active part of your daily management style.

Invite the Employee Into Your Office

Invite an employee into your office just to thank him for a job well done. Be sure to tell him why you believe he did an outstanding job. Don't discuss any other issue that will distract from this thanks. Involve him in the conversation by asking how he did such a great job. Ask if he likes what he is doing. Where does he want to be in the next year or two? Get to know him on a personal level. Ask how his family is doing. What did he think about last night's ball game?

Post It!

"Thank you" is one of the most powerful phrases in the English language. It almost always generates a smile from someone's face. Carry some Post-it™ notes in your pocket. Use them to put a thank-you note on an employee's desk if she is not there to verbally thank in person. Watch her favorable response once she finds you. The simple message could be "Thank you for your contribution in today's staff meeting."

Have the Boss Call

Everybody likes to be recognized. The higher up the level of recognition, the better someone will like it. Have your boss call an outstanding employee on your behalf and thank her for a job well done. Better yet, have your boss call and invite the person into the boss's office to deliver a personal thank you. You will double the positive impact on your employee if you're there too.

Wash the Employee's Car

Prove to all of your team that you're not afraid to get your hands dirty. Wash an employee's car in the parking lot to show your appreciation for a job well done. Don't tell your employee what you are going to do. Having your team bring the person out to the parking lot and surprise him. Enjoy the laughs you'll get. The goodwill will more than pay for itself.

Take the Employee Out

Everybody loves to go out for a free breakfast or lunch. Taking an employee out to eat is an excellent way to thank him for a job well done. Schedule the breakfast or lunch ahead of time so he can plan. Have fun while you're out and encourage the employee to discuss anything that's on his mind. He'll love you for it.

IN*sight*

You can excite your team by making informal
rewards a daily occurrence.

Make a Public Announcement

Modest people will tell you they don't like to be acknowledged in a public forum. This is a bunch of bull. Most people love public recognition. Hold a staff meeting and announce how proud you are of one of your employees for her outstanding job performance. Keep it secret so that she will truly be surprised. Award her a certificate or other token of your appreciation.

ONE-MINUTE PRAISING TECHNIQUES

Tell employees you are going to let them know how they are doing. Praise them immediately whenever they deserve it. Be specific about what they did right. Show how their effort is benefiting your organization. Always encourage employees to continue with their outstanding performance. Let them know about any problems.

IN*sight*

Always greet employees by their name when you pass their desk or meet them in the hallway.

LOW-COST REWARDS

There's a story about a Hewlett-Packard engineer who burst into his manager's office to anxiously announce that he'd just found a solution for a problem the group had been struggling with for weeks. The manager was so excited that he started groping around his desk for something he could give his employee to acknowledge the accomplishment. He ended up handing him a banana from his lunch bag. The two of them

PLAN OF ACTION

Spend a small amount of money on a clever informal reward and your dividends you will far exceed your investment.

had a good laugh as they ate the banana. The Golden Banana Reward became the most prestigious informal reward an inventive Hewlett-Packard employee could earn.

Create a Hall of Fame

Informal rewards are spontaneous. You never know when you are going to give one, but you are always looking for the opportunity. You want to do two things: give credit to your outstanding employee for her accomplishment and encourage the rest of your employees to excel.

Create a "Hall of Fame" with photos of your outstanding employees. Take a picture of everyone who receives an informal reward and post it on the wall. Add a photo collage that shows people working together on a successful project. Put these photos and records of achievement in

---

PLAN OF ACTION

Measure the success of every reward you give and make sure you give everybody an equal chance to win.

---

a scrapbook at the end of the year.

Add Continuous Support

Continuous and supportive communication from managers is too often overlooked. It's a major motivator. Small informal rewards take little time and can accomplish great things. Write a note on the envelope of an employee's paycheck to acknowledge an accomplishment. Leave a voice or e-mail message for someone thanking her for a job well done. You'll put a positive spin on the rest of her day.

RECOGNITION COMES FROM THE HEART

Compensation is what you give people for doing the job they were hired to do. Recognition is something you give when people do more than what's expected of them. Effective recognition must come from the heart.

RECOGNITION IS NOT OPTIONAL

Effective recognition is often a one-time event to celebrate a significant achievement or milestone. It must be planned in order to be timely and pertinent to the people you want to recognize. The Minnesota Department of Natural Resources found in a recent survey that recognition activities contribute significantly to employees' job satisfaction. The following are employee responses to some of the survey questions:

- A total of 68 percent said it was important to believe that their work was appreciated by others.
- More on-the-job recognition was desired by 63 percent.
- Only 8 percent thought that people should not look for praise for their work.

PLAN OF ACTION

Recognition is so easy and inexpensive to distribute that there is simply no excuse for not doing it.

SUMMARY

More and more employees say their job satisfaction depends not only on salary, but also on acknowledgement of their work performance. This is especially true of outstanding employees who are highly interested in their work and take satisfaction in their achievements. One of the best and easiest ways to acknowledge good work is by consistently offering your people informal rewards. Do this and you'll be rewarded with an outstanding team.

HOW DO FORMAL REWARDS HELP RETAIN OUTSTANDING EMPLOYEES?

F ORMAL REWARDS ARE OFTEN USED TO HELP RETAIN OUTSTAND-
ing employees. Several studies indicate that formal
rewards are not as effective as informal rewards.
Nevertheless, they should be an important part of any
reward program. Formal rewards are a good way to
acknowledge significant accomplishments, especially those
that span a long period of time. Formal rewards can also
lend credibility to more spontaneous informal rewards and
show your on-going commitment to your team.

FORMAL REWARD GUIDELINES

Formal rewards must be constantly monitored to
assure they are effectively motivating your employees.
Unlike informal rewards, formal rewards can become

obsolete in a relatively short time. For example, you may have a formal reward program to recognize employees who help you achieve a specific quality control goal. Once that goal has been achieved, the reward program terminates. A set of program guidelines will help focus on current issues.

Tie Rewards to Organizational Objectives

All members of your team should know your organization's objectives. If they don't, then you have to make sure everybody knows what your objectives are as soon as possible. Then you may announce a formal reward program that is directly tied to achieving these objectives. Formal rewards not only help reinforce the importance of organizational objectives, they also add an element of fun.

Make Sure Your Timing Is Right

Always schedule a formal reward as soon after an employee achievement as possible. Two things will happen if you wait or delay the event. The employee will think the reward isn't all that important, and you will also lose credibility with your other employees.

Promote the Value of the Award

Formal rewards typically have a higher financial and professional value than informal rewards. For example, a formal reward could be round-trip tickets for two to Hawaii or a significant cash bonus. One could say you don't need to promote the obvious value of this reward. However, if you post a glowing poster of Hawaii in the lobby of your company, you will triple the excitement for people who are trying to win the reward.

A professional attribute reward is subtler and may not carry an immediate dollar value. It may simply be a formal recognition in front of the executive staff for a job well done. However, it could catapult the winner's career far beyond what he would have gotten out of a free trip to Hawaii.

Always Present Formal Rewards In Public Forums

All formal rewards should be presented in a public setting. Schedule a special meeting if necessary. It's best if no one knows ahead of time who is going to get it. The suspense is part of the fun. Don't tell anybody of your final decision unless it is absolutely critical to the planning phase of the reward ceremony.

WARNING

If you think someone can keep a secret about a reward you plan to give, think again. Most people can't.

Don't Oversell Rewards

It's important to stress the benefits of your formal and informal rewards programs. But don't oversell them. Make sure your people know you expect outstanding performance on a daily basis. That's just part of their job. Rewards are what you give when they exceed such performance. That is something only you can define.

Make Sure Your Rewards Are Universal

Your formal rewards program must be flexible to accommodate employees' different needs and capabilities. For example, if you design a reward program strictly around achieving a sales objective, you are catering only to your sales people. This locks out the rest of your employees. Be sure to plan your formal rewards program so that everybody has an equal chance to participate in it.

———————————————— **WARNING** ————————————————

Always comply with IRS tax laws that govern
formal rewards programs.

SUMMARY

There are several ways your company can initiate formal and informal reward programs. Rewards are great ways to acknowledge your staff's accomplishments, especially if those accomplishments span a long period of time. Use informal rewards to help keep your staff perpetually motivated. Use formal rewards to help keep your employees focused on key organizational priorities and objectives.

HOW DO YOU SET UP ACHIEVEMENT REWARD PROGRAMS?

MANY COMPANIES TAILOR THEIR REWARD PROGRAMS TO FOSTER employees' specific achievements. These might include cost savings, outstanding customer service, or attaining company sales goals. Some achievement rewards are relatively easy to administer; others are more difficult. For example, how do you determine who is your most outstanding employee of the month when you have several to choose from?

OUTSTANDING EMPLOYEE REWARDS

Many organizations reward their distinguished employees. They may vote someone Employee of the Month or Outstanding Employee of the Year. Such rewards are generally based on a variety of formal and informal criteria. The reward is especially significant when both management and the employees participate in nominating candidates and choosing the winner.

Show employees how what they do makes a difference and is valuable to your organization. They will go out of their way to perform at a higher level.

START AN EMPLOYEE OF THE MONTH CLUB

Pick an "Employee of the Month" based on criteria such as high productivity, quality improvement, or meeting sales quotas. Display the employee's photograph in a prominent place. Honor the person throughout the month at special events. Then invite your employees to select one of these twelve "Employees of the Month" as "Employee of the Year." Create a special "Employee of the Year" reward and let everybody know what it will be to add excitement to the game.

IN*sight*

Outstanding employees love to have their performance measured. It helps them focus their sites on where they want to go.

PRODUCTIVITY REWARDS

Productivity rewards are used to encourage outstanding employees to maintain a certain level of productivity or performance. A recent study conducted by The American Management Association (AMA) confirmed that most employees want to be actively involved in improving there overall work performance. People tend to be satisfied, productive, and motivated when they are recognized and rewarded. An unrewarded employee may perceive that high performance is a dead end and slack off. Workers surveyed for the AMA study revealed the following:

- A total of 89 percent thought their companies would perform better if employees were given more quality and productivity goals.
- If management involved them in continuous work improvement efforts, 93 percent said they could do better against foreign competition.
- Only 40 percent believed that the average American company offers employees meaningful incentives to improve productivity.

WARNING

Poor performance should never be automatically rewarded. However, across-the-board cost of living or seniority increases are unrelated to performance.

EMPLOYEE SUGGESTION REWARDS

According to a recent article in the *Wall Street Journal*, less than half of America's work force believes their company listens to their ideas for improvement. American workers therefore make only about two work-improvement suggestions a year. This is in contrast to the average Japanese worker, who submits over a hundred suggestions a year. The American situation is unfortunate. In this age of increasingly complex work environments and mounting pressure to improve productivity, companies need all the help that they can get.

Eastman Kodak is one company that offers a great employee suggestion reward program. An employee whose suggestion is implemented receives 15 percent of Kodak's out-of-pocket savings. If a suggestion results in a new product, the person gets 3 percent of the first year sales.

DON'T FORGET TO ASK

When Donald Peterson, Ford Motor Company's CEO, started visiting company plants and talking with employees, he was reassured by his positive reception. One man told Peterson he had been with Ford for 25 years and hated every minute of it until one day his supervisor asked him for his opinion. From then on, he loved his job.

CUSTOMER SERVICE REWARDS

Satisfying customers is a goal all companies want to reinforce. Smart companies recognize employees who help them meet those goals. It costs a lot of money for most companies to win a new customer. That same customer can be lost in a matter of minutes due to customer service tactics.

Here's a simple customer service reward program you can implement. Invite customers to write the name of a particularly helpful employee on a coupon and drop it into a box. Give a reward to the employee with the most coupons.

Empower Your Customer Service Team

People want to feel empowered to find better ways to do things and to take responsibility for their own actions. Allowing employees to do this

EARN YOUR CUSTOMERS RESPECT, AND THEY WILL REWARD YOU

Fancy sales pitches, high-powered marketing strategies, and clever advertising campaigns are important attention getters. They may attract customers in the short-term. But keeping customers for any period of time depends on earning their respect, which is a key customer service responsibility.

will have a favorable impact on performance and increase their satisfaction with your company. This is particularly important in customer service, where the last thing an irate customer wants to hear is excuses. It's important to hire outstanding customer service people who can think on their feet and are able to resolve customer problems on their own.

HOW TO

Many organizations are trying to do more with fewer employees to create a competitive edge in today's business world. It's critical that such companies encourage and reward employees who can help them contain their costs.

IN*sight*

Employees who feel good about your organization
will give you their best on the job.

SALES GOAL REWARDS

One of the more easily quantifiable achievements in most companies is the attainment of sales goals. Sales reinforcement rewards are therefore common in most organizations. Morris Savings Bank in Morristown, New Jersey, has an innovative and successful sales reward program. They call it their Fast Track program.

Tellers are rewarded not only for landing new business, but also for cross-selling to existing customers. Each teller is allocated a quarterly quota of 45 cross-sale points. They earn a point for each additional service they sell to a customer and get a $2 commission for each sale. A sales coordinator tracks each teller's performance in the branch and posts the results in the lunchroom. A sales reward is given quarterly to the top teller.

Advanced Micro Systems, a manufacturer of computer chips in Sunnyvale, California, once mounted an all-out sales promotional campaign. Their goal was to reach $200 million in annual sales. The sales reward was a house, and every company employee got to participate in the contest. It didn't matter whether the person was directly involved in sales or not. All of their names were put into the hat for a drawing that would be held if the company goal was reached. Needless to say, the entire company was focused on reaching the annual sales objective. When they succeeded and the drawing was held, a factory-line worker won the house.

————————————— **WARNING** —————————————

Work on ways to include your non-sales people in reward programs. They may otherwise come to resent your sales group.

GROUP REWARDS

When a team of employees achieves a strategic company goal, each person needs to be recognized. Reward only the top performer and everybody else may lose motivation. You put together a team of bright minds to focus on a problem and come up with a solution. Everybody on the team needs to be recognized.

Take them all out to lunch. Then as they prepare to go back to work, tell them they can have the rest of the day off. If you can afford to, give each person a $100 bill and suggest that they use the money to go out and buy something they really want. You'll be a hero, and the next time you ask for team volunteers, you will be swamped with anxious candidates.

Darrell Mell, the vice president of Covenant House, stressed the value of involving employees in his company's decision-making process. "We encourage employee teams to provide input into all strategic decisions that are made so that they can share in the ownership of them. That way, nothing is forced on our employees because they're involved in the decision-making process."

INsight

People work harder when they know there is something in it for them.

LOOK FOR OPPORTUNITIES IN YOUR OWN BACK YARD

American workers have been telling us for years that the answer to increased productivity and motivation can be found inside their own companies. All managers have to do is ask the people who are doing the work. They'll tell you exactly what needs to be done. Offering them meaningful rewards at every level helps to accomplish productivity objectives.

TEAM REWARDS

Almost everybody you hire in today's entrepreneurial organization has to be a team player. A man in one of my seminars asked for an example of when you would hire an "outstanding non-team player." He put me on the spot to come up with a plausible answer, but I was able to provide one that satisfied him and my audience. The answer was to tell them about a man named Dale. He was a combined hardware and software genius who also had the personality of a cobra snake. Nobody liked him. If assigned to a team, he would tear the heart out of every member before the effort ever got started. But, if you gave Dale a one-on-one software challenge that included a reward and warned everyone to leave him alone, he would inevitably come up with a brilliant solution. That's what made him outstanding. He was a one-man team. But Dale was the exception. Here are six steps you can take to build team rewards into your organization:

1. Hire outstanding people who can work well with everyone. Ask them for ideas on what would be an exciting team reward.
2. Have routine one-on-one discussions with everyone on your staff. Try to avoid using structured meetings to solicit interstaff communications. Make it clear to the team that everybody wins if everyone works together as a team.
3. Hold informal retreats to foster communication and the exchange of ideas within your organization. Make the retreat both functional and fun. It could even be a part of your achievement rewards program.
4. Reward collective achievements whenever possible, even if it's just a pizza you buy for the group.
5. Pop in at the first team meeting and express your appreciation for everyone's involvement. Tell them about rewards you expect to make if the team meets its goal.
6. Send a letter to every team member expressing your appreciation for her contribution.

IN*sight*

Those who produce shall share in the results. Those who
stand by, content to watch, can keep on watching.

SUMMARY

Achievement awards offer you an opportunity to mobilize your entire organization to obtain a critical objective. An effective reward must offer something that everyone in your organization can get excited about. Remember how Advanced Micro Systems offered a home as the winning prize if the company achieved its sales goal. That sales goal was definitely met.

HOW TO USE CONTESTS TO EXCITE OUTSTANDING EMPLOYEES

C ONTESTS ARE A GREAT WAY TO BUILD ANTICIPATION AND momentum towards attaining organizational goals. But you must be specific about what one has to do to win. Contest rewards are often confused with achievement rewards. However, the two are actually quite different. Contest rewards are typically rewarded to an individual or an identified group of people (i.e., work team) who has successfully won the contest while competing against others.

Specific rules are in place to determine who wins the contest and participants know exactly what they must do to win. Say it's a "tug-of-war contest." Your team knows that if it can drag the other team into the mud hole first, it wins.

There are no ground rules for winning achievement rewards. In Advanced Micro Systems's case, everybody in the company had an opportunity to participate in the achievement reward (i.e., drawing for a house) as long as the company met its sales objective. The following is a review of the components that are essential to implementing effective contest reward programs.

CONTEST REWARD GROUND RULES

An effective contest reward program has to offer something that excites every employee who participates. This may vary widely in different organizations. Say your company employs mostly younger people, but you offer of a luxury liner cruise where the average passenger age is 65. It's not likely many of your people will get excited about winning the contest. Your contest reward must appeal to as many people in your organization as possible. You might try offering several rewards and let the winner choose the one he likes best.

PLAN OF ACTION

Tie the contest reward to the needs of your organization like improving customer relations. Iimproving the response time to customer requests for service calls could be one way to improve customer relations.

Set Realistic, Achievable, and Measurable Goals

Somebody has to win every contest you set up or you will quickly lose your credibility. Be sure the winning criteria are ones that someone in your organization will either meet or exceed. For example, if you say the first person to reach x number of units wins, but nobody reaches that number, your contest is a bust. Instead, tell your people that whoever has the highest number of units by a specified date and time wins the contest. This way you'll always have a winner.

PLAN OF ACTION

Select prizes for employees that have lasting value, inspire pride of ownership, and are useful.

Limit Contests to Short Periods of Time

No contest should last for more than thirty days. Beyond that, the people will forget what the contest was all about and will lose interest. Use contests to reward employees for accomplishing short-term objectives. You can always announce a series of contests to reward short-term accomplishments which are part of a long-term objective.

PLAN OF ACTION

Offer a special trip, like to a resort, to reward everyone who meets or exceeds a specific company objective.

Keep Contest Rules Simple

Be absolutely certain that everyone participating in the contest knows exactly what it takes to win. Otherwise you could have more than one employee claiming victory. Then you would either have to award multiple prizes or decide who won based on ambiguous rules. You will lose in either case. Your employees will lose confidence in the credibility of any future contest and may even leave your organization as a result.

PLAN OF ACTION

Ask as many as possible to review your contest rules. This will assure the rules are fair and easy to understand.

Link Contests Directly to Individual Performance

Track and field offers a classic example of how individual perform-ance is important in a contest. A 100-meter runner depends on herself to beat the rest of the pack to the finish line. If she succeeds, she wins the contest. There is nobody out there on the field that can say at the awards ceremony "I was responsible for helping this person win the race." A coach may be able to claim indirect responsibility. But only the runner gets the reward. When you present a contest reward to an employee, make sure that you are rewarding the person responsible for the accomplishment. If it was a team effort, reward the entire team.

PLAN OF ACTION

Give a raffle ticket to anyone who meets a contest objective. Then hold a drawing and award the winner a night on the town, a resort weekend, or round-trip tick-ets to Hawaii.

LINK CONTESTS TO TEAM EFFORTS

Hardee's Food chain holds an annual Competition for Excellence in which three people from each of its more than 2,000 restaurants compete. The teams are judged by regional and district managers on three basic qualifications: according to customer satisfaction surveys, the appearance of the food that they serve, and the cleanliness of each total restaurant. The regional and district managers periodically interview the various teams and submit their evaluations on how well the teams work together. Hardee's offers both regional and national rewards under this program.

IN*sight*

There's nothing wrong with giving away
money to a contest winner.

DON'T THINK THEY ARE ALWAYS HAPPY

Never tell your people they are simply lucky to have a job. At a time when employees are being asked to stretch themselves with fewer resources, you want to reward them as they stretch. Offer an exciting contest. Unusual sweepstake prizes draw great interest. There's nothing like a good contest to get sales cranking.

TRAVEL REWARD CONTESTS

A significant reward in terms of cost and planning is a trip to a desirable location. In a recent survey of American workers, 77 percent ranked trips with a spouse or guest as one of the most desirable possible rewards. Travel rewards have a number of favorable advantages:

- They are extremely popular.
- They are easy to promote and create lots of excitement.
- They foster team spirit and promote healthy competition.

Travel rewards do have their disadvantages. They cost a lot of money and take your employees out of the office. You can overcome part of this problem by scheduling trips on weekends.

> ——————————— **WARNING** ———————————
>
> *Travel reward programs can backfire. Someone who brags about*
> *winning the trip may cause other employees*
> *to resent your travel contests.*

SUMMARY

Again, contests are a great way to encourage desired behaviors in your employees. Describe desired behavior as well as other contest requirements, and make the reward explicit. Consider planning one of the contests described in this chapter to inspire your organization to help you meet your goals and objectives. Remember to select prizes that have lasting value, inspire pride of ownership, and are useful.

> **HOW TO**
>
> How do you create an inexpensive travel reward? Send an employee to a health spa for a day or weekend.

WHAT CAN YOU DO TO KEEP YOUR TEAM MOTIVATED?

T HERE ARE LITERALLY THOUSANDS OF DIFFERENT WAYS TO MOTI-
vate people. This chapter will cover just a few of them.
To inspire your team with motivation you must stay
close to its members. *Sports Illustrated* offered an interesting story in which an editor interviewed Fran Tarkington,
one of the greatest quarterbacks in the history of football.
During the interview, Tarkington recalled a play where he
had to block.

Blocking quarterbacks are about as rare as three-dollar
bills. Tarkington's Minnesota Vikings were losing to St. Louis
and he knew he had to call a surprise play to save the game.
Nothing would surprise the defense more than seeing
Tarkington become a blocker. The play worked when

Tarkington took out a tackler and his teammate scored the game-winning touchdown.

Bud Grant was the Viking coach at the time. When he came into the locker room after the game, Tarkington was waiting for his expected pat on the back. It never came. Grant praised everybody involved in the play except Tarkington. Tarkington confronted Grant in the privacy of his office and asked, "Didn't you see my great block coach? How come you didn't say anything to me about it?" Grant replied, "You don't need it. Yeah, I saw the great block you made. Fran, you're always working 100 percent out there. I figured I didn't have to tell you." Tarkington replied, "Well, if you want me to block again, you do!"

The moral of the story is don't ever take any of your outstanding team members for granted. If you're a team leader, keep your team motivated by touching each of your players at least once a day with praise and words of encouragement. If someone on the team is slipping, jump in and say, "What can I do to help?"

As you apply the following suggested motivational techniques, observe what motivates people you admire. This will sharpen your own motivational skills. Observe people's voice inflections, speaking manner, eye contact, facial expressions, posture, and self-confidence. Totally motivated people motivate not only themselves, but also everyone around them. Try to be this kind of person yourself. You'll be amazed at how much more productive you'll become, how easy it is to get help from others, and how motivated people around you will become.

IN*sight*

Always promote an "open door" policy to everybody in
your organization who wants to talk to you.

HOW DO YOU MOTIVATE YOUR TEAM?

All people possess a common set of needs and wants that when triggered, activate their respective levels of motivation and drive them to improve their current situation. There are six premises that you can apply to bolster a team's motivation. The following is a discussion of what these premises are and how to apply motivational tactics to get the most out of your team.

> A smile conveys an upbeat attitude about life. Frowns project the opposite. When you greet others with a smile, you take the first step toward showing your value and worth to that person. Every time you smile you promote yourself a little more.

Give Them a Reason

Every team must have a reason for what you want it to accomplish. Always take the time to explain why an assignment is important to your organization. Does everybody on the team understand the assignment? Tell them what you expect from completed assignments. Never assume that your communication skills are so excellent there can be no misunderstanding. Survey your team members and ask them the question: "What are the important objectives that we want

> **—— WARNING ——**
>
> *Keep your word and every promise you make to your employees.*
> *Otherwise they will never be motivated to*
> *do anything you ask of them.*

to accomplish on this team?" If you get consistent answers from everyone, you are ready to go. If you get divergent answers, you have problems.

Does Your Team Have Goals?

An effective team must have goals and objectives to sort through and work on every day of the week. Make sure every team player knows exactly what those goals and objectives are. Do they know what they have to do to achieve stated goals? If not, explain it to them.

To help assure the team's success, remove any barriers that may prevent it from completing assignments. Adjust individual job descriptions if necessary to fit particular employees' strengths. Empower and encourage all of your employees to join work teams. Also, make sure everyone who is working for you is having fun.

PLAN OF ACTION

Send key employees to a goal-oriented seminars to show them how interested you are in their personal growth.

What's Good for the Organization Is Also Good for You

Always set goals you believe are good for both the team members and your organization. Employees will lose motivation if they pursue goals that have no personal value. Say your team is working on a sales proposal that's critical to the on-going success of your organization. Offer career incentive rewards. Make it clear to your team that if your organization wins the proposal, everybody wins. Perhaps it will open new career opportunities. It could also have a positive influence on the next performance appraisals of the employees involved.

INsight

Teams will only pursue goals if they are motivated. The reverse
is also true. Teams with no goals to pursue
won't be motivated.

Make Sure Your Goals Are Attainable

Never assign a team a goal that nobody believes is attainable. Most people, no matter how valuable a goal might be to them, won't make the effort to go after a goal unless they believe that their chances of attaining it are good. For example, you may fantasize about becoming the company's president, but won't do anything about it if you believe that your education is inadequate to reach that goal.

WARNING

Never let outstanding employees remain frustrated
for an extended period of time. You'll lose
them to competitors.

MAKE YOUR TEAM MEMBERS JUMP AND SHOUT

Give an employee a thrilling adventure with a skydiving package that includes instructions and the first jump. Most packages include training, jump equipment, an instructor, the flight, and even a celebration lunch when you make it to the ground. Jump packages are relatively inexpensive and available across the country, particularly at small airports.

SUMMARY

Remember, motivation is the fuel that drives your employees to achieve outstanding performance for your organization. Without it, your organization will float around like a ship without a rudder. If you want to motivate your group, you must also be motivated. Try to fake it and you will lose—your employees will see right through it.

17

WHERE DO FRINGE BENEFITS FIT INTO YOUR REWARDS PROGRAM?

O NE OF THE PRINCIPLE REASONS PEOPLE LEAVE ONE EMPLOYER for another is to improve their compensation package. This motivation has existed for decades and will continue to be an influence as the work force becomes increasingly mobile. Employees, particularly outstanding ones, want to have something to show for their investment of time and energy at work. They want money to spend, money to save, and the security of a strong benefits program. The younger generation of American workers has become conscious of conspicuous consumption. They want to show what they have achieved through the acquisition and display of material goods.

IS MORE BETTER?

Many employees equate "more" with "better" and focus on the quantity of compensation rather than quality of the job they hold or work they perform. For some, compensation is the overriding issue. Others expect to be fairly compensated while enjoying a positive work environment. This is the case with most outstanding employees. You need to be sensitive to how your people feel about these issues in order to maximize the leverage you get out of your compensation package. The following are compensation ideas and options you can use.

RAPID FIRE CHANGES

The field of compensation is rapidly changing. Flexible financial packages, combined with creative benefit offerings, are heavily influenced by an ever-changing tax structure. What works today may not work or even be legal tomorrow. Today, you need compensation professionals to help you stay on top of the situation.

Offer Your Employees a Menu

The IRS has varying ways of taxing income. Some tax treatments are more favorable than others, depending upon people's personal status. Consider offering your employees a compensation package that's served up cafeteria style. This not only gives them a great deal of flexibility, but also gives them the opportunity to get the most bang for their compensation bucks.

For example, suppose life insurance is one of the offerings in your compensation package. An older employee with grown kids may not have much use for life insurance. Instead, that employee may elect to apply the cost of the life insurance plan to an IRA account. A younger employee with a new baby may want the life insurance plan.

Is Your Compensation Package Fair, Legal, And Dynamic?

A successful compensation program must be fair and legal and must appeal to everyone in your organization. If the program is overloaded with benefits that appeal more to young people, then it may not be fair. Has the program been reviewed by your attorney and accountant to assure that it passes IRS tax code and legal requirements? Are you able to change your compensation package to meet the needs of a changing mix of employees? For example, say you're initially hiring younger employees for your new start-up organization. Will they be interested in a different compensation package than employees who consider retirement and 401k plans more valuable?

PLAN OF ACTION

Make sure your employees know the full value of your compensation package, including the Social Security payments you contribute on their behalf.

PAINT THE BIG PICTURE

Unfortunately, most employees view their compensation package with a salary bias. Weekly or monthly take-home pay is the "big picture" in their minds. It is therefore critical that you take the time to show not only your outstanding performers, but every one of your employees, the full value of their compensation package. It's up to you to paint the real "big picture."

Here's how you do that. Create a list of all the benefits that are available to your employees. Next to each benefit, show its annual dollar value. For example, if you provide health insurance, show the dollar amount you contribute each year. For sick leave, show what it would cost you annually if the benefit was fully used. Make sure you include all of your government contributions for benefits such as Social Security, workers' compensation, and unemployment insurance. Costs for these programs vary from state to state, so be sure to adjust your figures accordingly.

PRESENTING INDIVIDUAL COMPENSATION INFORMATION

Create an individual compensation report for each of your employees and distribute it to everyone simultaneously. Do this at least once a year. Include a complimentary letter thanking your employees for giving you a year of their service.

OFFER INCENTIVE PLANS

One way to focus your employees' attention on maximizing their performance is by offering incentive plans. These plans may be designed differently for various job levels and functions. They may be based on accomplishing key strategies or on productivity or task performance objectives. All incentive plans have to be based on measurable results. They should also be designed on a unilateral basis to assure that all segments of your organization are covered. You don't want any of your employees to feel left out. Provide outstanding compensation for outstanding performance.

————————————————— **WARNING** —————————————————

Make sure employees covered under an incentive plan know exactly what they must do and how their results will be measured to win the reward.

Link Every Employee's Performance to Compensation

Linking pay to performance has long been an objective of compensation plans. Unfortunately, most are not well executed. One reason performance-based plans have failed is because employer and employee expectations have not been properly matched or understood.

Start by keeping it simple. Nobody, including your employees and managers, will understand a complicated plan. Develop realistic objectives that can be measured. Then define exactly how to measure each objective as well as the level of expected performance. Show what you consider to be unacceptable performance, what is expected, and what constitutes outstanding performance.

Cover the Details

Thoroughly communicate your performance plan to your employees by describing how performance is calculated and what rewards are paid for different levels. Show how employees can achieve outstanding performance and participate in the reward program. Be sure everything is in writing and signed by both you and your employee.

Give employees a copy of the signed document and keep the original in their personnel files.

HOW TO

Focus your performance plan on key issues that truly impact operations. Usually three or four issues are sufficient.

ADD A PROFIT-SHARING PLAN

Competition, mergers, cost reduction, organizational restructuring, changing technologies, and work methods have made it imperative that organizations rethink how they use their work force. More and more employers are approaching these issues with profit-sharing reward programs. Profit sharing has been around for a number of years, but its popularity and effectiveness as a compensation tool has recently begun growing rapidly. This is due in part to the entrepreneurial spirit of our economy and culture. Everybody wants to be an entrepreneur and start up his own business.

However, most of your employees either don't have the money or the knowledge to make it on their own. A profit-sharing plan offers them the best of both worlds: job security and a share in the entrepreneurial growth of the company.

Why Is Profit Sharing Popular?

Profit sharing is popular because it is simple, its measures are understandable, and everybody—from the lowest employee to the company's owner—has a stake in profits. Make a profit and everybody gets to keep her job and the investors in the company are happy. Profit-sharing plans include both immediate cash payout plans and deferral plans. A payout plan pays cash to eligible employees at the end of a stated period of time, typically at the end of the company's fiscal year. A deferral plan can take many forms. The company could make deposits on behalf of employees into their IRA or 401k plans. Deferral plans can have tax advantages for employees.

How Do You Implement a Profit-Sharing Plan?

Most companies will establish a minimum profit they must achieve before beginning profit sharing. For example, say a company sets a threshold of 10 percent profit. It then establishes a profit share percentage of 50 percent for all profits above the 10-percent threshold. Profit-share funds are deposited into a trust account on behalf of the employees. These funds are distributed to employees at the end of the performance period either as a fixed amount of cash or a percentage of their base salary.

COMPENSATING WITH TRAINING

Many companies faced a dilemma as they entered the new millennium: a scarcity of skilled workers. This means you may have to hire people with high potential but minimal skills. Skill-based compensation systems work best when employees participate. The more employees know about their work, the more productive and valuable they are to you.

By participating in a training program, an employee has an opportunity to learn, to become more productive, and to get paid for it. Make sure a new employee is clear about the skills that need to be acquired. Agree on a time frame for starting and completing the various parts of the program. Record everything that you have agreed to in writing.

What Are the Objectives of a Training Program?

Training programs can offer your employees a broad range of opportunities. The basic objective of any training program offer is to encourage your employees to improve upon their job skills so that they can do a better job for you. That's a reasonable objective when you consider that you are paying for either part or all of the training. Your training program could include taking specific management-approved courses in a discipline the company deems important. It could also include giving your employees the opportunity to earn a higher degree by paying college tuition.

How Do You Implement Training Compensation Programs?

Suppose you hire a potentially outstanding employee at a base salary that's less than what it would be if he had the skills you need. During the hiring process, you and the employee agree on a plan to develop his skills. The plan might go something like this: If he takes and completes the classes you agree he needs, then you will increase his salary by a mutually acceptable amount. The employee takes the classes during his off-work hours, and you pay the fees for the classes.

IN*sight*

Offer high-potential employees who are short on skills additional compensation for completing skill-based training and education.

OFFER YOUR EMPLOYEES AN ESOP PROGRAM

ESOP stands for "employee stock ownership plans." These plans enable employees to acquire stock in publicly traded companies where they work, usually at preferred rates. Employees who have ownership in your company tend to be significantly more interested in its growth and success. They'll also be more committed. The compensation benefits of ESOPs can be significant. They enable your employees to accumulate retirement funds or money for a down payment on a new home. They also have a tax deferral advantage. Assuming the stock appreciates, employees don't have to pay any capital gains until they sell the stock. ESOPs provide an added incentive to stay with your company and experience its growth and success.

WARNING

ESOPs work best for companies whose stock has a progressive history of going up. If your stock doesn't appreciate, or worse yet, loses value, an ESOP can actually ruin motivation.

SUMMARY

Fringe benefits are an important part of any total compensation package. They are even more important than salary to some employees. Monitor the effectiveness of your compensation program on a regular basis to make sure it is serving all of your employees. Flexible benefit programs are becoming more popular with the rank-and-file worker. You may want to consider this in your own organization.

18

HOW DO YOU MOTIVATE OUTSTANDING EMPLOYEES?

T HE POTENTIAL POWER OF HUMAN MOTIVATION IS AN AMAZING thing. The journals are filled with stories of people who triumphed against unbelievable odds. Think of Helen Keller who became blind, deaf, and dumb as a toddler, but grew up to become a successful author, lecturer, and advocate for the disabled. Motivation, along with self-awareness, imagination and conscience, is among the most important human endowments required to achieve and sustain high levels of productivity.

Notice the use of the word "sustained." You can temporarily increase productivity by applying short-term techniques such as fear or cash rewards, but you can only sustain productivity with ongoing motivational techniques. Take away people's motivation, and they lose their drive to do anything but the bare necessities. As you read about the following motivational situations, concentrate on understanding the human issues behind motivation.

—————————————————— **WARNING** ——————————————————

Dr. William Mayo, founder of the famous Mayo Clinic, once said, "Lord, deliver me from the man who never makes a mistake, and also from the man who makes the same mistake twice."

COMMON MOTIVATIONAL DRIVES WE ALL HAVE

One basic premise of motivation is that people generally fall into one of four personality categories. First, you have the power players who like to take charge of everything they do. Next are the team players who love to work with anybody on anything. Then come the diplomats who will do anything to avoid a confrontation. And finally, there are the party players, those gregarious people who like to have fun at whatever they are doing. Each of these personalities usually responds best to different motivational techniques.

Despite personality differences, all people share three common motivational drives. First, people have reasons for everything they do. They do not act blindly, but will set up goals in their never-ending attempt to get what they want. Second, people are generally selfish. They'll choose to do something because they believe it is good for them. Although their behavior is directed toward goals, each goal must offer something good or it will quickly be discarded. And third, the goals people choose to pursue must be attainable. No one chooses a course only because it has value to them. If they discover their goal is not attainable, they'll stop pursuing it.

WHERE DO YOU FIT IN?

All managers are in the unique position of being able to offer goals that will motivate their employees. You have the opportunity and responsibility to increase your employees' expectations of reaching their goals and enhancing their personal situations. This is the essence of good management. It's also the fun part of management and should drive your enthusiasm and personal motivation every day. There are numerous roles you can play to motivate everyone around you. Good managers recognize that their success is directly dependent upon the success of outstanding people who work for them. And that depends largely on how effectively managers apply motivational techniques.

IN*sight*

Assignments that may exceed an employee's capabilities are OK and
can drive her motivation. The key is that you both agree
to take on the challenge.

What Influences a Person's Motivation?

This is a good place to review some of the principles that are behind staying totally motivated. Mangers have the assigned responsibility to motivate everybody who has an influence on the success of their organization. Managers can accomplish this task only if they are totally motivated themselves. Motivation is influenced by three primary factors: personality types, their perception of the person who is trying to motivate them, and their desire to achieve meaningful goals.

WARNING ———————

*You can break down employees' motivation by giving them
assignments that have impossible barriers
or exceed their capabilities.*

What Motivation Factors Do You Need to Consider?

A manager's success as a motivator depends on how well she is able to apply the basic factors of motivation. Understanding and recognizing the employee's personality characteristics is critical. For example, the approach you take when addressing a person with a power-oriented personality should be considerably different than the one you'd take when addressing a person with a diplomatic personality.

Your choice of motivational techniques depend on your employee's perception of a situation. If you're discussing a problem that she created, is she willing to take ownership of the problem? To find out, ask her probing questions. Does she know what needs to be done to solve the problem? She may honestly not know. You need to be prepared to step in and offer a solution they can accept. Always follow up to assure the motivational techniques you employed are working.

Motivating a Person to Accept Change

We also know that people's reaction to change depends on several factors. Employee's attitude toward change can determine whether they are either motivated or demotivated by the proposed change. Their values or what is important to them influences their understanding of what they need to do to become motivated. People's perceptions of what others will think if they do or do not change also influences their ability to accept change.

MAINTAINING MOTIVATION THROUGHOUT YOUR ORGANIZATION

To maintain motivation throughout an organization, totally motivated managers don't just talk; they walk-the-talk through the hallways and into every crevice of their organizations. Motivated managers always demonstrate by examples that others can see and touch. Your consistent enthusiasm, drive, and relentless pursuit of goals all set the tone for motivation throughout your organization.

Day-to-Day Interactions

Day-to-day management revolves around a series of human interactions that require the use of different motivational techniques and strategies. These strategies depend on your understanding of how people think, what turns them on, and what turns them off. You must constantly be aware of everyone who touches your organization. How are your people feeling? Learn all you can about them by asking them questions, listening, and observing.

MOTIVATE EVERYBODY YOU TOUCH

Instill the practice of motivation into your management style. You'll be amazed at how productive your people will become, how easy it is to get others to help, and how totally motivated you'll become in the process.

Keep On Observing

Always observe more than what people around you are saying. Watch for changes in their voice inflection, speaking manner, eye contact, facial expression, posture, and self-confidence. Once you are confident you understand a person and know his personality type, seize the opportunity to motivate him now. Don't wait until tomorrow or allow distractions to get in your way. A totally motivated manager motivates everyone who can help improve the overall performance of the organization.

PLAN OF ACTION

One of your greatest challenges as a manager is to find ways to motivate your people and keep them motivated throughout the workday.

--------------------- **WARNING** ---------------------

Loose lips can sink motivation. Be very careful about talking
behind people's backs. If they find out what you said,
it can have devastating effects on
their motivation.

IN*sight*

You cannot manage men and women into battle,
but you can lead them.

GIVE PEOPLE REAL WORK TO DO

Outstanding employees hate busy work. They'll do anything to avoid it, perhaps even quit. They want to be engaged in exciting and productive work that challenges their innate talents. The more you can link assigned tasks to productive mission-oriented results, the more motivated people will be to do the job.

CLASSIC WAYS TO DEMOTIVATE EMPLOYEES

Never criticize or humiliate employees in front of their peers. Never reject their ideas without providing a good reason. Never give assignments people do not understand or fail to provide them with a realistic career path. Never assign people to teams where they are not a good fit.

Watch Out for Downtime

When you develop a work schedule, try to balance it so that none of your outstanding employees encounters a period of downtime while waiting for others to catch up. In case that happens anyway, don't wait until the last minute to deal with it. Create meaningful tasks for idle workers that you can assign on a moment's notice.

PLAN OF ACTION

Train your employees to always look for something to do when they have time available. Give them ideas or a list of things to do if things get slow.

Give Them a Break

Don't push too hard. There are times when it is wise to let your people take a well-deserved break. Let them relax for a few minutes once work is caught up to show your appreciation. It's not necessary to push your people every working minute of the day. Balancing breaks with work can actually increase employees' productivity. It will also keep them motivated.

SUMMARY

Your success as a manager and entrepreneur depends on how well you develop relationships within your organization. If you don't effectively motivate your people, you will see substandard performance in everything they do. This chapter discussed a variety of ideas for motivating people. Always be cognizant of what you do and say, and how it affects the motivation levels in your organization.

HOW CAN YOU GET MORE OUT OF YOUR OUTSTANDING EMPLOYEES?

I F YOU WANT TO GET MORE OUT OF YOUR OUTSTANDING EMPLOY-ees, you must first capture their attention. In his book *Presentations Plus*, David Peoples contends that 75 percent of what people know comes to them visually, 13 percent comes from hearing, and 12 percent comes through smell, touch, and taste. This means presentations that include visual aids, such as pictures and graphics, create more lasting impressions than simply words. Information that is seen has a much greater chance of being remembered than information that is heard.

SPEAK WITH A VISION THAT PEOPLE CAN SEE

Use words to paint a picture when you're speaking. This will help employees understand exactly what you're trying to communicate. I recently attended a dinner party sponsored by the Society for the Prevention of Cruelty to Animals (SPCA). The president delivered an excellent message by creating a vision that was the theme of his speech. "Imagine yourself alone and starving. You're on a cement street surrounded by cement buildings. The buildings have no doors or windows. The street is endless and there is no hope. That's what a lost or abandoned cat or dog faces when it's turned loose in the city." Try to create a similar vision when communicating a strategic assignment to one of your outstanding employees. You want her to picture in her mind exactly what needs to be done and why it's important to the organization.

Use Descriptive Words

Descriptive words will help an employee see as well as hear what you're saying. Say you are about to assign one of your outstanding employees to a fact-finding team to explore alternatives to high fuel costs. Here are two sentences that basically say the same thing. Which one would you choose?

1. High fuel costs have had a bad effect on our company.
2. The cost of fuel is increasing, and like an acid, it's eating away our company's bottom line.

The first sentence is dull and boring. It leaves no picture in your mind. The second sentence is only six words longer, two of which are action words, yet it helps paint a picture of what's really happening. It should be easier for you to listen to and assimilate the second sentence because there's a graphic element to it. You can visualize the problem through the words. Imagery words are useful in all types of daily communications.

Don't Be a Broken Record

How many times have you heard the boring words from the airline flight attentdants "Please keep your seat belts fastened until the plane comes to a complete stop." I remember one stewardess saying, "If you'd like to not suffer the embarrassment of falling down in the aisle, please keep your seat belts fastened until the plane comes to a complete halt." Her added comment got a good laugh and the passengers stayed seated.

The use of descriptive words helps you paint a picture for your listener. Words create images, and whether you're talking about a dog, the budget deficit, or seat belts, you can make your message colorful, interesting, and memorable with imagery. Using imagery in a message is one of the most enjoyable parts of making a presentation. It forces you to be creative.

COMMUNICATE THROUGH YOUR HEART

Have you ever talked to someone who was looking at you straight in the eye, but afterwards you realize he didn't hear a word you said? You knew the person was not listening because his eyelids were struggling to stay open or he had a glazed look on his face. I've had this happen to me and wondered why. Then I finally figured out it was my fault. Although everybody knows you hear with your ears and see with your eyes, I had only been talking to people's ears. Their eyes decided they had nothing to do with the conversation and they subsequently closed. To be an excellent communicator, you must learn to not only speak to the ears of your listeners, but also to their eyes. Why the eyes? Because the eyes are the key to opening one's heart.

Make a point first to people's ears, then to their hearts by using an illustration. Watch their eyes light up. You'll know you have helped them see with their heart what they have just heard with their ears. Their lips will curl up as they smile in recognition. Then rush back to their ears again to register another point. This is the art of successful communications that you must learn to develop.

You must learn how to communicate to an employees' eyes, ears, and hearts, or you'll find yourself out in left field. Another great way to communicate to people's hearts is with humor. Everybody loves to laugh and humor paves the way to heartfelt communication. Hearing the truth can be boring, but hearing it with humor can produce warm recognition from the heart.

One of the classic ways to introduce bad news is by asking, "Do you want me to tell you the good news first, or the bad news first?" The bad news will definitely capture the listeners' ears. The good news will capture their heart.

FIRST THE BAD NEWS

At a recent board of director's meeting, the chairman announced: "The bad news is we've been taken over by XYZ Corporation." Everybody in the boardroom heard what the chairman said with their ears. Then he said, "The good news is the acquisition offer includes a 25 percent increase in our current stock price." Now he had captured the hearts of all the stockholders. Try to get people to think with you by personally involving them in what you're saying. You will be well on your way to becoming an excellent communicator.

Make Your Point

Remember the old saying "It's not only what you say to your team but how you say it that counts." A soft or squeaky voice when you are trying to make a point could cause you to lose credibility and even your audience. Always deliver a presentation to your team with confidence mixed with a healthy bit of humility. No one likes to listen to an arrogant speaker in a team environment. If you can make your employees feel comfortable with you and your communication style, you'll win their admiration every time.

Draw a Picture for the Team

It's essential when speaking to a team that you adjust your communication style to accommodate the different personalities of all members. As a rule of thumb, make short, concise statements to get your point across and follow up with questions like "Does everyone understand what I just said?" Whenever possible, use pictures to illustrate your message. If pictures or illustrations are not available, paint the picture with the appropriate words.

WHAT THE EXPERTS SAY

The National Speaker's Association in Tempe, Arizona, has been working for several decades with professionals at all levels to develop outstanding communication skills. Many association members make over 100 formal presentations a year to audiences all over the world. According to the National Speaker's Association, there are ten ways to turn people off when you talk to them. Some of these are:

Monotone Voice

Have you ever watched hypnotists in action? They start talking to their patient in a very deliberate, slow, monotone voice. In less than a minute, their patient is sound asleep in a hypnotic trance. We have all experienced the same thing at a lecture where the guest speaker started talking about a potentially exciting subject in a monotone voice. If it wasn't for our spouse or friend who was sitting next to us and constantly jabbing us in the ribs, we too would have fallen asleep. The point is, never use a monotone voice when you are talking to your employees. It will be impossible for them to get excited about whatever it is you want them to do.

Don't Read Your Material

Employees will assume you don't know what you're talking about if you read your material while making a presentation. If you knew, you wouldn't have to read the material off a dummy list. It's OK to refer to notes, but keep your eyes off the paper and focused on your employees as much as possible.

Don't Be a Bore

If you sound boring and uninteresting when you talk to an employee, you can rest assured that they will walk away from the conversation with the same feeling. Allow that feeling to persist, and you won't get much out of them on the next assignment. Try to make every assignment, even the boring ones, as exciting as you possibly can. Here's an approach that might help you get started. You tell John, one of your outstanding employees, "John, I have an assignment to give you that quite frankly is not very exciting. However, you are the only one I can rely on to get it done." You have created some excitement in the assignment by telling John "he's the only one."

Make Sure You're Prepared

Good preparation is critical to maintaining an open channel of communications with an outstanding employee. Rambling, getting sidetracked, and having unorganized material will all block that channel. Always remember that outstanding employees pride themselves on being well organized. Discovering they are working for someone who is not well organized may cause them to question your ability to help them reach their career goals and objectives. They may also start looking for another job.

Don't Use Annoying Body Language

Never use annoying body language such as fidgeting, swaying, and arm waving when you are addressing employees. People will immediately see that you are nervous about whatever it is you're trying to communicate. They will give more of their attention to watching your body language than listening to what you're saying.

Don't Be a Repeater

A person who repeats the same thing over and over attracts attention for all the wrong reasons. If you are talking to employees like this, their first reaction might be to wonder if you're not losing your mind. You have already told them what you need. Repeating may also indicate self-doubt. For example, your employees may wonder whether you are sure of your authority.

Make Eye Contact

You've heard it said before. If you don't look at people you're talking to directly in the eye, they will immediately sense that something is wrong. They will quickly conclude that you are either lying or completely unsure of yourself. Eye contact is an important part of body language that was covered in an earlier chapter. There are all kinds of subtle body signals you can send when communicating with your employees, but there is nothing subtle about not maintaining eye contact. People will notice immediately and discard whatever you have to say as fast as they delete junk mail.

You Must Relate

You must relate to your employees if you want them to have an effective communication line with them. Relationships in the business world are built on trust.

WARNING

Never try to hide undelivered commitments from the rest of your team. The news will spread like wild fire throughout your organization.

Remember the western movie *Sheep Man* with actor Glen Ford? Ford played the role of a sheep man confronted with a situation in which his relationship with the cattlemen was on the line. He made a deal with them and cemented his relationship by holding out his hand. "My handshake is as solid as my word," he said. "You can bank on that." Make sure you deliver on every commitment you make to your people. If you are ever unable to deliver on an employee commitment right away, tell the person why you were not able to honor your commitment.

ALWAYS BE A WINNER

In every thought you have, act you perform, and in everything you say, you have the choice of being optimistic or pessimistic, positive or negative. Rest assured that the optimists are always more successful at getting what they want than are the pessimists. An optimist is prepared and confident. Being an optimist also helps set you off from the rest of the pack. Your employees will pick up on your optimistic attitude, and the overall productivity of your organization will grow.

GET YOUR OUTSTANDING PEOPLE INVOLVED

One of the best ways to get more out of your outstanding people is to actively involve them in the internal and external workings of your organization. They will gain a greater appreciation for the challenges you face and see their role in meeting those challenges. Be sure you show your top performers how they can grow as your organization grows. The following are several ways to get more effective use out of your outstanding employees:

Invite Them to Participate

Everybody likes to be invited to an event, even if the person doesn't want to go. Most outstanding employees will be delighted to participate in a company-sponsored event if you invite them. Here's why. You will demonstrate that you not only trust them to make a good presentation, but that you want to expose their talents to your organization. What a great way to indirectly communicate your confidence in outstanding employees.

Send Them to Trade Shows

Sending your best employees to trade shows where they can rub elbows with their counterparts in competitive companies will increase your exposure in the labor market. Of course this assumes the people you send are loyal to your organization and fully understand their mission at the show. A trade show also helps employees see where your industry is going and how they can help you get there.

Pass Their Knowledge on to Others

Your outstanding people have knowledge that is essential to the growth of your organization. It may be in sales-closing techniques, production control methods, or the finesse of handling irate customers. Encourage these people to pass their knowledge on to the rest of your team. Ask them to conduct an on-site seminar during lunch or after hours. Reward them with extra money for their time or offer them a night out on the town for two. Most outstanding employees will jump at the opportunity to show what they know to their fellow workers. They'll also appreciate that you recognize they have expertise in certain areas worth sharing.

HOW TO

Show your top performers how they can grow within your organization. Help them establish personal goals.

Leverage Their Strengths

All outstanding employees have a good perception of their strengths and weaknesses. They will openly discuss their self-improvement plans for minimizing their weaknesses and building their strengths. Unfortunately, most of them don't have a coach to help them fine-tune their self-improvement programs. That's where you can step in and offer your coaching expertise. You will often be able to point out strengths people didn't know they had as you help them overcome their weaknesses.

KEEP IMPROVING YOURSELF

Everybody in today's business world could be happier and more successful if he really wanted to. Why then are so many people unable to accomplish this? Somewhere along the line, they have stopped improving themselves. They have become complacent and unwilling to take the initiative to improve. More important, these people are not willing to learn how to do new things to increase their value to their organizations and themselves.

Invite Them to High-Level Company Meetings

Outstanding employees generally love to attend high-level company meetings. It reminds them that they too are aspiring to higher-level positions. When you invite outstanding employees to attend high-level meetings, you are indirectly giving them a vote of confidence. After all, you wouldn't invite just anyone

Invite Them to Speak at a Company Event

Outstanding employees welcome the opportunity to demonstrate what they know to others. They are proud of their accomplishments.

Invite them to speak on a subject they choose at a company event, such as the Christmas party or even a staff meeting. The invitation in and of itself will reinforce to them your sincere appreciation of their qualifications.

Ask Them to Help You Recruit New Employees

Encourage outstanding employees to help recruit new employees. This is a win-win situation. It allows your new job candidates to meet and chat with your best employees, which increases your odds of attracting new people into your organization. It also sends a signal to your outstanding employees that you trust their judgment enough to allow them to participate in recruiting.

SUMMARY

All of the tactics covered in this chapter will help you communicate effectively with your outstanding employees. Not all your communications have to be verbal. Communicating through actions, such as inviting employees to attend high-level meetings with you, can reinforce your loyalty to them.

20

WHAT DOES THE FUTURE HOLD FOR YOUR ORGANIZATION?

J AMES IS A FORMER CEO OF A MEDIUM-SIZE MANUFACTURing COMpany who's spending his retirement years in bitterness. I first met James in his spectacular executive office when he was a CEO. He struck me as a pompous man who reveled in being a big frog in a small pond. I arrived at his office a few minutes before our appointment and was leafing through the company's magazine when I noticed that he was featured in the magazine's lead article.

The article described James in almost messianic terms and praised his management style. According to the article, his keen incisiveness, gruff exterior, and bluntness marked his "excellent" management style. I learned from the article that one of his favorite gambits when anyone presented him with a new idea was "Are you ready for a grilling on your idea?" A few minutes later when I met with him to review my proposal, he used those exact words, "Are you ready for your grilling?"

I have always believed that a potentially good idea can't come about unless it is discussed openly. Moreover, if the discussion is to work, it has to be done in an objective environment. My problem with James was that he took such glee in grilling the merits of any idea presented to him. He was so busy grilling that he never heard any of my good ideas. The communication was all one-way, with James acting as both judge and jury. I believe he enjoyed the fact that everyone who approached him did so in a state of terror.

I later found out why James had retired in bitterness. Unbeknownst to him, his entire executive staff met privately with the board of directors and demanded his resignation. Their request was honored that same day. James suffered from change paralysis. He wouldn't listen to any idea involving change and was paranoid about what changes the future held. This story is a reminder of how important

---

INTERESTING RESULTS FROM A MANAGEMENT SURVEY

In *Forbes* magazine's annual corporate survey last year, 90 percent of the companies admitted their management was reluctant to change. One of the exceptions was Tassani Communications. The company encourages managers to spend time with other managers on a regular basis. They are given the option of selecting a peer manager to shadow or having the group's executive pick one for them. Managers follow a peer around for a day and learn what she does. This helps them broaden their own perspective about change. As Tassani's vice president put it, "It's a great way to get everybody in the company involved in the changes that are occurring throughout our company, it doesn't cost a lot of money for the program, and it encourages support between managers."

---

it is to hire people who love to change as the needs of your business dictate and who are willing to listen with an open mind to any and all ideas.

EMBRACE CHANGE

A highly regarded systems engineer at Hewlett Packard told a newspaper columnist: "I feel threatened. The life cycle of a product around here is less than six months and if I can't keep up with the pace, I'll be a veritable antique before I reach thirty." Today's skills, knowledge, and products live fast lives and die young. People are being asked to learn quickly and produce more with less money at a laser-fast pace.

"Change is happening faster than we can keep tabs on it and change threatens to shake the foundations of America's most secure corporations," warned a recent study by the U.S. Congress's Office of Technology. No industry will escape it and no one is exempt.

Be Prepared to Adjust

Today, as change accelerates in every area of our lives, the conventional thinking that guided us in the past is outdated. It's clear yesterday's wisdom won't work in today's turbulent environment. A vivid example of what happens when you stick with conventional wisdom occurred in the early days of football. In 1905, football was a low-scoring sport of running and kicking the ball. A bunch of guys in leather helmets would line up and see if they could push the other team back for a three- or four-yard gain. A four-yard gain was a big deal.

When the forward pass was legalized in 1906, it was suddenly possible to gain 40 or more yards with the flick of a wrist. But, most of the teams stayed with their conventional running games that first season. Recognizing that football had entered a new era in which the three-yard strategy was obsolete, the coaches at St. Louis University adapted quickly and switched to a forward-passing offensive game. They outscored their opponents 402 to 11.

Change Is Challenging

Each day companies face changes that are as challenging as the forward pass was to football almost a hundred years ago. Every time you turn around, the rules of the game have changed. You can no longer afford to recycle, modify, or revise the conventional wisdom of the past. The pace of change in the new millennium will make the past look like a cakewalk in the park. Tim Nelsen, an enlightened friend of mine, told me, "The time to change is when you don't have to, when you're on the crest of the wave, not when you're in the trough." Tim and I used to surf at Santa Cruz, California, when we were in college together.

In an environment where waves of change are coming from all directions, Tim's metaphor is right on. Keep changing while you're ahead of the wave by initiating required action in your organization. Don't get caught in the trap of just paying lip service to change, or you'll never catch the wave. You'll be just another observer standing on the beach watching all the action out in the surf. The future belongs to those who know how to make change happen before anyone else knows what's going on.

IN*sight*

Ben Franklin once said, "We must all hang together, else
we shall all hang separately."

PERSPECTIVE ON THE FUTURE

Some people say it's impossible to predict the future. Others argue that the past is prologue. Historians caution that those who do not study the past are doomed to repeat it. Economists tell us that everything moves in cycles. Seers suggest that the future is now. Futurists talk in terms of trends.

Given all this wisdom, one might suppose you really can predict the future. One can join the futurist and study the trends, while accepting input from the seers and economists to determine the future and how it will affect business organizations. Based on today, and our recent past, you can predict with a fair degree of assurance, the immediate future. It gets a little shaky if you try to predict beyond a couple of years. What will employees want three to five years from now? What will an outstanding employee look like in terms of qualifications in five years? Will you be able to recruit employees the same way you do today?

Employees of the Future

Outstanding employees will continue to be the most vital resource for nearly every kind of organization that produces goods and services. Some low-end jobs will remain about the same, but most other jobs will change dramatically with the rapid introduction of new technology in the workplace.

The knowledge and skill base of the average employee will change in response to both technology and the need to produce more with

---

NEW TEACHING MODELS

A new generation of college graduates with teaching degrees will begin working in the industrial sector. They will teach a wide variety of technical and personal development skills that are either not offered or are inadequate in the public education system. Companies will have to provide this educational support if they want to capitalize on the potential of their people.

---

fewer resources. A smaller work force, with a changing composition, will be called upon to keep the machinery of the economy working. This will present a frustrating challenge for managers as they compete for the best people they can find.

Changing Work Attitudes

Good attitudes will regain their importance in the workplace and in other aspects of employees' lives. Attitudes will spell the difference between outstanding employees and your other employees. A new type of training called "attitude training" will be offered by many companies that are interested in converting good employees into outstanding employees.

Attitude training will help some employees discover their real potential. For others, it just won't work. They will find it difficult to overcome the counterproductive attitudes that some people learn over the years.

INsight

People with poor attitudes will wonder ignorantly why
the world is passing them by.

People with the Right Stuff

Outstanding employees who are blessed with the "right stuff," like a positive attitude and good technical skills, will be even more successful than they are today. Their attitudes will be even more highly demanded in the future. The demand for such people will almost assure the fulfillment of their career dreams. They will have a wide range of job opportunities, so you'll need to be even more aggressive in searching for future outstanding employees.

> **HOW TO**
>
> To attract outstanding employees of the future, create innovative ways to attract them that your competitor hasn't thought of.

FUTURE LEADERS

Soon there will be no managers working in dynamic organizations. Unless you are a proficient leader, you won't be allowed to direct the activities of other people. Old hard-line management techniques simply won't work or be accepted in future organizations. All outstanding employees of the future will also be outstanding leaders.

Unfortunately, precious few people in management today know how to be leaders. Managers will have to know and practice a whole new set of skills if an organization is to excel. Colleges and universities are already adding leadership classes to their management programs to help fulfill this need. Other organizations will provide skill training to help managers work and lead more effectively. Most training will focus on team leadership, sales, and customer service.

Management training will focus on how to develop a highly flexible organization where every employee is focused on delighting customers. Instead of acting like a herd of sheep, they'll become more like a flight of self-directed geese flying in formation. Every employee will know the common direction and goals of the organization, is willing to assume leadership when necessary to get there, and can quickly adjust the structure of the organization when the needs of the customer demand it. Individuals start doing their jobs better not because some manager orders it, but because they want to excel. In other words, managers who are also leaders encourage their people lead to achieve new levels of excellence.

THE FUTURE OF THE SALES ORGANIZATION

Sales and customer service will be even more consumer oriented in the new millennium than it was in the past. Sales will be based on long-standing relationships in which professional sales executives will help customers buy what's best for them, including a product or service from another company. Service after the sale will become increasingly important in all sales fields as companies compete to attract new customers. Outstanding people who know how to leverage the full strengths of an organization to obtain a sale will be in high demand. Customer service will become a major part of the sales organization and will extend far beyond smile training. The customer of the future will expect higher quality in both merchandise and service.

FUTURE ROLES AND STRUCTURE

In the future, employees on the front lines will be expected to accept greater responsibility in getting a job done. Accountability and authority will extend from senior management right down to hourly employees. This will be inevitable as companies thin out their management ranks.

Middle managers will become obsolete. They'll be replaced by computers and technological tools that will take over administrative functions. The remaining good managers will move into specialist positions where they will provide support for fellow team members. An enhanced sense of cooperation will replace the current fiefdoms that many staff and line departments have become.

More Freedom for Outstanding Employees

Outstanding employees will have more freedom to determine how to do their work. The emphasis will be on results and collaboration, rather than on activities and departmental independence. While outstanding people will be hard for some employers to recruit, others will have their pick. The difference will be in your company's reputation. For example, how well do your people work together, and what opportunities do they have to grow in your organization?

Embrace Changes

The changes that the future brings will be comfortable for some organizations and painful for others. Some organizations are already adopting strategies and changing their business models to capture the essence of the future. Many other companies are having difficulty changing and some will not change at all. Most inflexible organizations will disappear just as the dinosaurs did two million years ago. Montgomery Wards refused to change, and they're out of business.

IN*sight*

The future belongs to those who do what
needs to be done.

SUMMARY

Business is on the threshold of resurgence. You have the opportunity to enjoy the thrill of riding the wave into the new century. The knowledge you need is already here. By now you know what you need to do to attract and keep outstanding people.

The new millennium will offer some exciting challenges for every organization. Employers who can attract and keep outstanding people will become magnets for more outstanding people. Working together with a common vision and dedicated leadership, these teams of conscientious people will enjoy being on the leading edge of change.

WHERE ARE THERE MORE IDEAS TO ATTRACT OUTSTANDING EMPLOYEES?

T HERE'S A WEALTH OF GOOD BOOKS THAT ADDRESS VARIOUS facets of attracting and retaining outstanding employees. The following is a discussion of the material in some of the better books that are on the market.

Ways to Motivate People

If you get a chance, read *1,001 Ways to Inspire Your Organization, Your Team, and Yourself* (Career Press, 1998) by yours truly, David Rye. It literally includes over a thousand ways to inspire and motivate people in different kinds of business settings. You'll also learn how to recognize the four personality types that people have and how to apply motivational techniques that work best for each type.

Ways to Motivate Yourself

If you need more ideas on motivation, read Steve Chandler's *100 Ways to Motivate Yourself* (Career Press, 1998). Chandler covers the bare essentials of what it takes to get yourself motivated and then stay motivated most of the time. There is a lot of substance in this book.

Teaming By Design

Teaming By Design (Irwin Professional Publications, 1995) by Donna McIntosh-Fletcher shows you how to consistently get the most out of any team effort. Your ability to hire outstanding team players is essential to the success of your organization. The book will help you learn quickly how to create dynamite teams.

Live to Win

Live to Win (Harper & Row, 1989) by Victor Kiam shows you everything you need to know to win in business and achieve success. Kiam was the man who bought Remington, the shaving company, several years ago. His book is full of great examples of how different companies used their outstanding employees to obtain a variety of organizational objectives. It's easy to build an outstanding organization if you have a bunch of winners working for you.

Body Language

Body Language in the Workplace (McGraw-Hill, 1991) by Julius Fast shows you how to use body language to make a point. It also teaches how to read other people's body language to help you understand what they are thinking. As has been pointed out, knowing how to read body language can tell you a lot about a candidate in an interview. Fast shows you how to use your own body language to influence others to do what you want them to do.

Just Say a Few Words

Just Say a Few Words by Bob Monkhouse (M. Evans & Co., 1988) is filled with great ideas on how to effectively communicate. His ideas will help you capture the attention of outstanding candidates when you interview them. If you can't do that, you will never get them to join your organization.

Keeping Good People

Keeping Good People by Roger Herman (McGraw-Hill, 1991) presents literally hundreds of strategies you can apply to reduce staff turnover. Herman covers everything from environmental, compensation, and growth strategies that are relatively easy to implement. He also addresses how your leadership style can help your retain your outstanding employees.

Hiring Top Performers

Hiring Top Performers by Bob Adams and Peter Veruki (Adams Press, 1996) is a comprehensive directory of over 600 interview questions to ask candidates. It includes questions to ask for a specific job, such as an accountant or systems analyst. The emphasis of the book is on helping you qualify candidates.

Rewarding Employees

Bob Nelson's *1001 Ways To Reward Employees* (Workman Publishing, 1994) covers a wide variety of reward programs. It's filled with hundreds of examples of successful reward programs that different companies have used to increase the overall productivity of their people.

Make Your Point

To learn more about how to sell your ideas, read *How to Get Your Point Across in 30 Seconds* (Washington Square Press, 1991) by Milo

Frank. It's must reading for anybody who is trying to attract outstanding candidates. If you can master the art of getting your point across in a matter of seconds, you are on your way to successfully recruiting outstanding people.

SUMMARY AND CONCLUSIONS

G EORGE FOREMAN ONCE SAID, "YOU ONLY FAIL WHEN YOU GIVE up." When you know in your own mind that you have given something your best effort and it's not working out, don't quit. Simply start another project. Years ago, a friend invited me to join him in a start-up business to sell a gadget that we were convinced millions of people needed. It didn't take me long to discover that nobody wanted our gadget and I got out of the business just in time.

My friend unfortunately tried selling our gadget until the bitter end and lost several thousand dollars in the process. When it was all over, he told me, "You know Dave, I hate to lose money, but the thing that really concerns me is that this experience will make me overly cautious. I'll be afraid to consider other viable business opportunities. If that happens, then my loss will be multiplied many times over." How true.

One man didn't let that happen. He was initially involved in an oil venture that ran out of money and oil. So he started a clothing store, which didn't do any better. He went broke, but he wasn't discouraged. It was later on in his life that he got involved in politics. Today, historians speak highly of Harry S. Truman, the two-time failure who kept getting back up and became president of the United Stated.

As you continue your journey to move your organization to the top, remember that each rung in the ladder is placed there to hold your foot just long enough to allow you time to step up to the next higher rung. It isn't just a footrest. Jo Lewis said, "Although we all get tired and discouraged when things are tough, you fight one more round if you want to be the champion. A second wind isn't good enough. You'd better have a third, fourth, or as many winds as it takes to win."

There's enormous potential in each person. But it's worthless unless you know it's there, how to use it, and even more important, how to find the right people to help you make it all happen. You must find, hire, and retain outstanding people if you want your organization to grow. Your persistence and effort are vitally important to your recruiting campaign. Good luck hunting for outstanding people!

INDEX